Teaching Drama: Fundamentals and Beyond

A System Using more than 250 Exercises, Improvisations and Activities

Thomas Crockett

ISBN-10: 069225403X
ISBN-13: 978-0692254035

Dedicated to the many brilliant students who helped develop and shape the ideas in this book.

TABLE OF CONTENTS

There was an Old Lady
Tiger, Tiger
Repeats with Vowel Rhymes
Control, Discipline, Focus, Concentration
Pronunciation Drill
Sentence Changes
Projection Practice using Poetry Lines

Two-Person Mirror
Mirror using Parallel Lines
Mirror using Parallel Lines with Directions
Mirror with Four Leaders
You Can't Break My Focus
Large Group Mirror
Small Group Mirror
Neutral Position Breathing
Breathing, Adding Arms
Breathing, with Sway
Breathing with Energy Squeeze
Dissolve, Drain, and Renew
Guess the Mirror Exercise Leader
Guess the Changing Statues
Eight Movements, using Mirror and Repeats

Learning Gibberish Rules
Practicing Specific Actions in Gibberish
Practicing Tone in Gibberish
Practicing Clarity in Gibberish
Large Group Gibberish Translation
Learning Genre Rules
Practicing Genres in Pairs
Techniques for Speaking Dialogues
Adding Words to Status Cards
Voice-Over Pantomime using One Speaker
Voice-Over Pantomime Changing Speaker
Outer/Inner Emotions
Emotional Transformations
Switching Emotions

Learning to Give, Take, and Share
Practicing Give, Take, Share in Pairs

SECTION II:
Short Dialogues

#1: Do you understand what I'm saying?
#2: Hello
#3: Hello. I was expecting you.
#4: This is my favorite thing to do.
#5: Why are you doing this now?
#6: I can't believe you're suggesting such a thing!
#7: I've always wanted to do this.
#8: So, here we are.
#9: So...
#10: Are you sure we can do this?
#11: Are we ready for this?
#12: Now, you're absolutely sure you know...
#13: Before we go ahead and do this, I need...
#14: Aren't you excited to go out and start your day?
#15: I am so excited, aren't you?
#16: Get up! I'm not kidding this time.
#17: Did you hear that?
#18: I can't believe we're doing this.
#19: Holy smoke! Look at that, will you.
#20: Get away from me.
#21: This has to be the funniest thing I've ever seen...
#22: Oh, my god, I can't believe what I'm seeing.
#23: If you do that one more time, you will be in trouble.
#24: My gosh, you're so clumsy.
#25: Holy smoke! This is the greatest!
#26: It's over between us, and this time I'm serious.
#27: I just can't do this anymore.
#28: Don't come near me.
#29: Look at me.
#30: You don't understand what I'm saying, do you?
#31: Oh, my god, what is that?

#32: Stop telling me to calm down.
#33: Wow, I've never seen the sky look so blue and clear!
#34: You are the funniest person I've ever met in my life.
#35: I can't do it!
#36: Get up, now!
#37: Is it my imagination, or am I hearing...
#38: Stop it!
#39: I did it!
#40: I feel so strong today.
#41: Isn't this just the most beautiful day?
#42: We can do this, I know we can.
#43: Why don't you ever help me around here?
#44: Are you ready to do this?
#45: Oh, my god, look at the stars!

SECTION III:
Improvisations

House Improvisation
Six Characteristics
Eight Characteristics
Two-Minute Drill News Program
Sentence Repeat, 30 Seconds
Using the Same Sentence Often
Using the Same Word Often
Adding Nouns
Piano Pantomimes
Piano Musicals
The Reverse
Closing Line
World Famous Therapist
Three Tables Related Stories
Outrageous Late-for-School Excuses
Classroom Experts
Classroom Emotions
Classroom Genres
Customer Service Return

Ending Photograph
The Magic Prop
First Two Lines
First Three Lines
Three Emotions
Make a Drawing
Emotion and Location
Jake and Jim
Judgement Day
Pantomime to Music
Music Stories
Songs with Themes
Single Prop Never Before Seen
Trying to Win the Hand of the Prince/Princess
Mannerism Interviews
Interview with Seven Characteristics
Subconscious
Storytelling Vowels
Storytelling Consonants
Storytelling Patterns
Two-Person Gibberish Translations
Three Tables Gibberish Translations
Alphabet Improvisation
Alphabet Line
Rhyme Improvisation
Rhyme Line
Environmental Switches
Car Mimic
Shared Mannerisms in a Revolving Scene
Freeze Tag
Freeze Tag, adding Students
Freeze Tag Reverse
Emotion Arms
Emotion Arms Mimic
Emotion Mimic
Props used Imaginatively
Props used Literally
Using Costume Accessories
Give Me that Chair
Give Me that Prop

Same Character Storytelling
Switching Emotion Storytelling
Word Tennis
Genre Storytelling
Genre Pairs
Two-Person Mimics
Group Story Gibberish Translation
Group Gibberish Song
Three-Person Gibberish with Host
Gibberish Poem
Voice Over
Can't Say I, Me, My, Mine
Questions Only
One Knows, One Doesn't
The Host and Audience Know, but the Guest Doesn't
Party Guessing Game
The Dating Game
Beginning Line
Speed Alteration Scene
Opposite Emotions
Same Situation, Different Emotions in Pairs
Two-Person Contrasting Motivations
Two-Person Conflict Tag Team
Language Translation
Playing Cards Status
Guess the Speaker's Status
That's Not What Really Happened
The Movie Theater
Mr. Know It All
One Scene Ends in Tragedy
Character Switches
Situation Switches
Sound Effects
Simultaneous Experts
Animal Characterizations
Limited to a Single Phrase
History Switches
Telephone Narration
Revolving Scene, adding Characters
Evolving Emotions

Secrets
Telephone Rumors
Audience Determines What Happens Next

SECTION IV:
Small Group Improvisational Scenes

Therapist Flashback Scene
Film Reviews using Genres
This is Your Life
News Show
Fortune Cookie Scene
Titles
Situational Titles
Emotion Statue
Same Scripted Story told in Different Genres
Slide Show
Moogie Mock
Story using Three Randomly Selected Words
Imaginative Use of Props
Wax Museum Figures
Time Machine
Meet Your Neighbors
The Reunion, using Dramatic Irony
House Improvisation Scene
Emotion Storytelling
Improvisation Contest

SECTION V:
Beyond Assignments

Foundational Speaking Practice

INTRODUCTION

I wrote this book with a clear understanding of what it's like to be given the responsibility to teach drama in a school environment. I imagined myself 23 years ago and the many unsettling questions that came into my head. I'm sure they're the same questions any new drama teacher would have: How do I teach drama? What, specifically, do I do in my class day after day, for 180 days? How do I engage my students, while cultivating and sustaining interest? These are big questions. To answer them, a teacher new to the profession, or one with limited experience, needs help. Therefore, I wrote the book I myself would have liked to read 23 years ago.

What I present in this book is a system for teaching drama. I did not invent this system overnight. Whatever I've written here comes from experiences I've had over a 23-year period teaching at the same high school. It took me nearly 10 years of teaching and learning before I implemented this system and its many ideas.

Year after year, I evaluated and revised, and that's the way it should be, because just as learning is a seemingly endless process of discovery, teaching is no different. Looking back on my early teaching experiences, I borrowed ideas from many excellent books written by teachers who had been working for 20+ years in the classroom. I borrowed freely the many exercises, activities, games and improvisations they wrote about, and I am grateful to them. In time, I learned to modify others' ideas and develop my own. The process takes time, however. If you're a new teacher or have relatively limited experience, understand that your process of growth, discovery and confidence takes time. Borrow freely and modify, as I did, and in time you will develop your own style of teaching, complete with original ideas and lessons.

While I am a high school teacher, I do not believe the information in this book is exclusive to grades 9-12. The ideas, exercises, improvisations and assignments are universal to drama, no matter the age of the participants. I also do not believe you have to follow the exact sequence of exercises or activities presented here. You should receive and process this information and modify accordingly, to suit your personality, the personality of your students, and the general needs of your class. Still, however you use this book, I caution you to have, at the very least, a general sense of a long-range plan. While the exercises, improvisations and assignments in this book have value in any sequence or context, their greatest effectiveness comes from knowing how they're connected and where they lead in terms of understanding and performing drama. With that said, there is a reason to my system and why I divide the book into five sections. This reason will be fully explained in the pages that follow.

However you use this book, I wish you luck in your teaching endeavors and hope the information in this book will benefit you and your students.

T. Crockett

SECTION I:
Large Group Warm-Ups, Exercises, and Activities

SECTION I: FOREWARD

While the ideas in this book can be extracted and used in whatever way the reader deems desirable, I recommend imperatively that Section 1 be followed and completed before the reader/teacher moves on to what I call the "Beyond" stage. What I do the first thirty days is ostensibly more about the subsequent 150 days. The reason is simple: the first 30 days create the foundation for the type of class I want for the rest of the year. What I hope to communicate here is that while considering and using each exercise, you keep an eye on the big picture, the entire year, and what you want your students to accomplish. To get to where you want to go, and want them to go, you must teach foundational exercises, such as you will find in Section 1.

The teaching of these exercises helps to establish and cultivate what I call the Group Soul. I do not mean something Emersonian or Transcendental. I am referring to a group of students who are unified and coherent; a group in the same space, at the same time, joined by a collective spirit and energy. The group exercises detailed in this book are designed to nurture the Group Soul. If you succeed in cultivating it, you will have found the guiding principle of your class. It will not only enrich your life and the lives of your students, it will contribute to making your drama class an exciting place of learning and profound personal growth.

Before I start with the exercises, here is some foundational information about how I manage my class from the start, because the exercises are limited without proper structure: The first day, I do not talk about the class. I do not talk about requirements, rules, procedures or grading. In fact, I do not talk. I direct. Immediately. I want my students to do drama, not hear about it. I assemble them in a large circle (I am fortunate to teach on an actual theater stage) and tell them to get used to this format. They will not be sitting in chairs for a long time. They will always begin in the large circle, and they will move and use their voices. They will not need textbooks, pencils and paper.

They need only themselves, fully engaged in the present, in the moment. They need only their fun-loving, yet disciplined, young minds, bodies and imaginations. If they bring these characteristics and take direction, they will learn exponentially.

I am their director, I tell them. To have a successful class—for them to learn and do drama properly—they must listen and follow my directions, and my directions must be clearly explained. This relationship between teacher and student is the most fundamental and important component of teaching drama, or anything, I suppose. Make sure the rules of the exercises, and all subsequent exercises, are clearly explained. Never assume they understand you, and do not proceed until you are certain they know exactly what to do. And this means you must know what you want them to learn. If you're not sure, they won't be sure, and the exercises will be exercises in futility and little more. You must treat and respect each exercise as if it's the most important exercise you will ever direct and they will ever do. They must be present, and they can only be present if you are, mentally and physically.

I divide the exercises into sections, though I do not teach one section at a time. I integrate them all on a daily basis. Use your discretion and common sense in determining which exercise precedes or follows another. They are all effective in their own way, in different circumstances, at different times, with different students. What unifies them is they are all large group exercises, involving everyone, at the same time, inspiring each student to buy into the program and engage himself fully into this interactive communication we call drama. Here, then, are the exercises for Section 1.

MOVEMENT WARM-UPS

1. Moving to Rhythms

I tell the students they are going to move, counter-clock-wise, staying in the circle. They cannot talk or make sounds. This is a "movement only" exercise. I count out rhythms, using numbers, varying the speed as I do so. They coordinate their movement with the rhythms, the speed. I start simple: 1, 2, 3, 4, repeated over and over. When I stop, they freeze. When I continue, they continue. These are the instructions for this exercise. I am fortunate and blessed to have one or two student assistants in each of my classes. I use them to demonstrate, for it helps if the students see for themselves what you want them to do. Since freezes are an essential part of the early exercises, I have my assistants demonstrate perfect and imperfect freezes. I want everyone to know what a freeze looks like. It is not something approximate, not 90%. It is exact, precise, completely unmoving. Make sure you follow through with your instructions and with your standards for how the exercise should be performed. You must establish your standards from the start. Otherwise, the students will never take your exercises seriously. If someone is speaking as he is walking, make sure you stop and re-emphasize the instruction. If someone is moving when he should be frozen, make sure you stop and point out the requirement for the exercise. Do not settle for "most" of the students are following the directions. Everyone must follow the directions, as given.

At this time, I mention the Group Soul. I want them to know these words. I want them to understand their importance. I want them to know that each person in the circle is connected with everyone else in the circle. Drama is not math or history. Individual achievement is not valued here. Group achievement is valued. Each student needs each other student. The circle exercises must be done in unison, in cohesion. Everyone must be in the same place, at the same time. This is also a time I mention the words that are the core foundation of my class: control, discipline, focus, and concentration. Learning and growth cannot take place without an appreciation and development of these skills.

In this exercise, I want to make sure they are taking and following directions. If I count fast, they move fast; if I count slowly, they move slowly. If I stop, they freeze. I start with a simple 1, 2, 3, 4, but I quickly change the sequence and the pattern. Use your imagination here. Infinite patterns exist. It's your choice where the direction of the exercise goes. In fact, so much of teaching drama is dependent on spontaneity, personality, imagination, communication, motivation, wit, power, conviction, and authority. I can give you ideas and exercises, but you must rely on these essential drama-teacher characteristics to help you take ownership of the exercises and of your teaching.

2. Move, Greet, and Freeze

This one is also a movement exercise, which also incorporates freezes. The difference is this one allows for speaking as well. I have students stand in a circle, and when I give the signal, I direct them to walk and converge in the middle of the stage, shake someone's hand, whisper their name to the person, and then move to someone else.

That's it: walk, meet someone, shake hands, and whisper their names to each other. Limiting their speaking to whispers is critical if I want the students to hear my directions. Sometimes I say freeze. Sometimes I call out an emotion. For instance, I might say, "exaggerated smile." In this scenario, students walk, greet each other with an exaggerated smile while they shake hands and whisper their names. If I say freeze, they freeze with their exaggerated smiles, still holding each other's hands. As with the previous exercise, I keep a watchful eye, making sure everyone is following the directions as given. If not, I stop. Now, someone might say, "But it's the first day of school; students are going to be shy and uncertain and a little awkward." True. Nonetheless, standards must be established and upheld. Immediately. Sure, some students will struggle because many young people do not come equipped with focus and listening skills, and the ability to take direction. True, true and more true. The greater the reason to teach them properly, I say.

For this exercise, it's important that the students spread out as much as possible. I will go through as many as ten emotions in this exercise. Of course, I want the students to interact with others, meet others. Some may call this an icebreaker. I don't call it that. I call it a drama exercise because it requires concentration, listening, freezing, and using and expressing emotions, both verbally and nonverbally. The second part of this exercise, I focus more on the movement. I give directions, such as the following:

- Walk crooked, greet, shake, whisper, and freeze.
- Walk on one leg, greet, shake, and freeze.
- Walk backwards, greet, shake, and freeze.
- Walk with legs together, greet, shake, and freeze.
- Take big steps, greet, shake, and freeze,
- Take small steps, greet, shake, and freeze.

My directions for an exercise like this are typically not premeditated. I rely, as I do for all exercises, on the spontaneity of the moment. I draw energy from the students and allow that energy to dictate my directions. The point of the exercise is this: use your spontaneous imaginative flow to develop ways for students to meet each other, and, at the same time, develop skills they will need and use in your drama class.

3. Clap and Stomp Patterns

Here is one I like to use on a daily basis, at the start of class. I use this one to get everyone in the same place, at the same time. It's a unison exercise, involving clapping rhythms and synchronized movement. I tell the students I am going to perform a clap and stomp pattern. Their task is to follow along with me once they figure out the pattern. Here's an example: 1) single clap, followed by a single stomp with my right foot. 2) single clap, followed by single stomp. 3) double clap, followed by single stomp. 4) single clap. I do it once or twice. When students figure it out they join me. I recommend using only simple patterns with this exercise. It's a unison exercise, not a trick exercise. The objective is to get everyone in sync, not confuse them. Now, of course, I can perform this clap and stomp in any variety of rhythms. Often, I'll use the same pattern, changing the speed. Try several patterns at the beginning of each class. It's a good way to say "Good morning, class" without speaking. After they put their bags down and join me in the circle, I begin. I clap; I stomp. They understand class has begun. Immediately, they are engaged; their blood begins circulating; they become involved in "doing, not thinking." It's primal, it's tribal, and it's musical. It's a language of the morning, and it speaks to the Group Soul.

4. Directed Physical Movements

I direct my students how to walk. Once again, I emphasize that this is a "movement only" exercise. Talking or interacting in any way is not allowed. I tell them that as they walk, I will ask them to place their energy on their arms, legs and hands. I tell them to begin walking counter-clockwise, and as they do, I add directions: "Rub your hands, shake out your hands, swing your arms, take large steps, take small steps, walk on the balls of your feet, walk with your knees leading, walk with your stomach leading, walk with your head leading, walk quickly, walk slowly." (Note: I don't give these directions in rapid succession. I usually change the direction every ten seconds). I vary this exercise by suggesting characters such as the following: walk like a toy soldier, walk like a person on stilts, walk like a cowboy who just got off a horse, walk like a 600-pound wrestler, walk like a fashion model. As I wrote earlier, much of what I do relies on spontaneity and imagination. I don't carry around a definite list of character or situational walks. I make them up on the spot. Allow yourself some freedom when you're in the moment. The suggestions I'm providing are just that, just suggestions. What's important is that the students are moving, using their bodies freely, while being disciplined, taking directions, and, of course, having fun.

5. Movement to Storytelling

I tell a story and direct students to move counter-clockwise around the stage, acting out what I say. This one is primarily a "solo, movement only" exercise (though, at times, I may have them repeat words that I say). While speaking is involved, the exercise is never, at any time, interactive. Students must stay in their own spaces, in their own imaginations, and not become distracted in someone else's. If, at any time, students begin interacting with one another, I stop to re-emphasize my instruction, to ensure everyone is together and unified.

I'm not going to write out the story here, because it's something I make up in the moment. I will, however, give you an example of what it might sound like: "You are standing near your door, you take your jacket from the closet and put it on. You open the door and step outside. You look up and say, "Ah, what a beautiful day." (The students say this line and all subsequent lines that I speak.) You begin to walk, and as you do you swing your arms. You are happy; you are smiling. Suddenly, you stop; you look up at the sky and say, "Oh, no, the sun has disappeared." You resume walking, only now you are dejected, sad. You stop and lift your hand to the sky. It has begun to rain. You remember suddenly that you have an umbrella in your back pocket. You take it from your pocket, open it, and resume walking, holding your umbrella. But the wind picks up. The umbrella is becoming hard to manage; it is blowing inside out. You are trying to hold on to it, but it is beginning to blow away. And then it is taken from your hands. You stop, watch it fly into the cold, rainy sky. Meanwhile the rain is pelting your head. You bear down, brace yourself as you continue walking, wiping the rain from your eyes. You stop, look up and spread your arms to the sky and say, "Let it rain on me, let it rain!"

At this point I can make the story as imaginative and fantastical as possible (and I often do). The students by now are involved, using their imaginations, walking and playing freely, while all the time listening, taking direction, involved in a drama experience which requires them to exercise control, discipline, focus and concentration. Each student interprets the direction a little differently, but that's to be expected. Even though the circle is made up of individuals moving and acting, the Group Soul is evident.

How long do I spend on this exercise? It changes every time I do it. Some days the story can go on for nearly 15 minutes, some days 5 minutes. It depends on my imagination and the collective focus, energy and discipline of the students. It's drama; it's live and immediate, so there's no way to predict from moment to moment the exercise's growth potential. I will say this: I must be attentive, aware and engaged. I allow the "moment" to dictate whether I continue or discontinue.

6. Moving to Increased Speed

I count to 30. As I begin, students walk counter-clockwise. I start slowly, gradually increasing the speed. As I increase, they increase their movement. No two numbers are the same speed; their walking speed is never the same. It is constantly changing. Not only is this one is a good warm up exercise to get the students' blood circulating, it also gets them to coordinate their movement with time, rate and speed. Sometimes I count in reverse, starting at 30, really fast, gradually decreasing the speed.

7. Moving to Sounds

I direct students to move with coordination to sustained sounds I make. The sounds, with distinct tones and emotions, elicit in their imaginations how they should walk. I might repeat, in a menacing tone, "bump, bump, bump, bump" or repeat in an innocent tone, "wee, wee, wee, wee." The sounds I make come spontaneously from me. I don't plan what I'm going to say or how I'm going to say it. What's important is that students are, once again, warming up their bodies and imaginations, coordinating sound and movement.

8. Zig, Zag, Zigger, Zoogey

The title may sound bizarre, but it's fundamentally a sound, movement and freeze exercise. I walk around the circle, point to students, giving them one of the words, in sequence (zig, zag, zigger, zoogey). If there are 36 students in my class, each word has a group of nine students, the first of whom is the leader. The leader says the appointed word and simultaneously makes a movement. The leader then freezes. The second leader has the next word. Then the third and fourth leaders speak their words, with accompanying movement and freeze. Then like dominoes, the rest of the students continue around the circle: zig, movement, freeze, zag, movement, freeze, zigger, movement, freeze, zoogey, movement, freeze, until we have completed the circle.

It's very important that each person freezes after his sound and movement, so that by the end of the circle, all the zig people are identical, all the zag people are identical, and so forth. This one—as is true for all the exercises—has no margin of error. It has to be technically and mechanically sound, and performed seamlessly.

9. Crazy Walks

Here's another warm up exercise I use at beginning of classes to help the students loosen up and free themselves from the cobwebs they gather during the school day, and in life, generally speaking. I have one of my assistants lead this one. I tell him to use his entire body when he walks: arms, hands, legs, feet, back, neck, head, etc. It's a crazy walk, after all, and the more body parts moving, the better. He walks in the inner rim of the circle. I tell the rest of the class to watch all his moving parts closely because when I count to 5, I want them to walk exactly the same way. I count to 5. They begin. I count to 10. I say, "Freeze." I count to 5. I say, "Unfreeze." I call on another student to do a crazy walk, and we repeat the pattern. Sometimes I allow the walking student to make an accompanying sound—a single, sustained sound—and have the rest of the class make this sound as well when they mimic him. I usually have the class perform five or six crazy walks, after which they are loose and ready for their day of exercises.

10. Moving to Increased Speed, Connected

This one, on the surface, may seem identical to the previous increased speed moving exercise. Yes, I count from 1-30, starting slowly, gradually increasing speed, and, yes, the students move accordingly to the speed. The variation, however, is that now I have them hold hands in the circle while they move, counter-clockwise. Though a quick exercise, in terms of time, it is significant in meaning, for this one requires advanced concentration and discipline. Not only must they listen carefully to the counting, they must stay together at all times, while not speaking or interacting with one another.

11. Pantomime Movement in Pairs

For this exercise, I add an interactive element. I have the students in the large circle divide themselves into pairs. I tell students I'm going to call out an action or a situation. I want them to work together. It's essentially a pantomime activity, where the students will imagine themselves in this situation and act accordingly. For instance, I might say, "The two of you are carrying a heavy couch, moving it down a flight of stairs." I might guide them through it. "Lift it, feel how heavy it is, take small, careful steps, watch your step, etc." Next: "You are folding a sheet." Or, "You are moving a refrigerator into your kitchen." You can come up with any number of activities that two people can do together that involves nonverbal actions. This exercise engages their imaginations, their senses, gets them working together, in silence.

12. Creating objects in Groups

I do a similar exercise in larger groups. I divide the class into groups of five, and tell them as they walk around the circle to stay in their groups, separate from the others.

When I call out an object, I instruct the students to stop walking and become the object. In other words, they must form their collective bodies and create a visualization of the object. I give them ten seconds from the moment I call out the object. This exercise does require the students to communicate. Here are some objects I might call out: a pencil being sharpened; scissors cutting paper; a canoe tipping over, a tree blown by the wind. When I count to ten, they freeze and hold their positions for another ten seconds. At that time, I have them resume their walking around the circle until I call out the next object. This exercise is a nice change from "movement only" walking. It allows for creative and spontaneous decision making, the students working together and thinking as a unit.

13. Creating Photographs in Groups

Here's something else I add to the daily group walks and movement: I have students walk in groups of five or six. This time I don't have them create objects. I have them create improvisational photographs. As the students walk in the circle, I call out a picture (for instance, "Body Builders") and count to 5. The students create a collective photograph and freeze. After I unfreeze them, they continue to walk, until I call out another picture. It's not hard to come up with photographs. Just about any suggestions will work, such as Chess Club; Rock band; Family portrait; Drama team, etc.

14. Move Like a Machine

Here's another exercise that isolates specific body parts while utilizing sound and repetition. It's a standard machine exercise, and it can be done in small or large groups. Students must look and act like a part of a machine. To do this successfully, they must believe completely. This one requires freedom, imagination, and total absence of self-consciousness. I direct students to use both their upper and lower body when they move, and they must also add a sound, a repetitive, machine-like sound. I have an assistant demonstrate because this one really needs to be modeled.

Here's what the large circle exercise looks like: one student starts; three seconds later, the student to his left begins; three seconds later, the student to his left begins. This pattern continues until everyone in the circle is moving and sounding like a part of a machine. This is not a mimic exercise. Students must create their own movement and sound. As much as anything else, this is a concentration exercise because students must be locked into what they're doing and not allow themselves to be distracted by the movement and sound around them. It requires absolute commitment.

If you have 36 students in the circle, and you feel it might take too long to go around the circle, you might try this variation: have the first five or six students follow the pattern, and then on the count of 3, have the rest of the circle, simultaneously, begin their machines. I, personally, do not favor this format. I find it's more chaotic, less clean and clear. However, there's no reason without proper conditioning and practice that it shouldn't be effective. As always, you should modify all these exercises to suit your personality and the personality of your students.

15. Pantomime Activity

I have everyone stand up. I hold an imaginary glass. I ask the class, "Does it look like I believe I am holding a glass?" I hear "Yes." "That's what it takes," I say. "I must believe if I want you to believe." I instruct them to hold a glass, to believe. I observe; I am satisfied. I tilt my glass, open my mouth, and swallow. I instruct them to do the same. They do. I tell them I am going to give them 42 pantomime directions. I assure them I will speak slowly and allow space and breath between each direction. Their task is to perform these actions believably as I give them. They must exhibit discipline, control and focus. Their movements, one at a time, must be clean, clear and precise. Their eyes must be absolutely locked in place. I give them the setting: they are in front of a bathroom counter, about to put on deodorant. Here are the directions, outlined in 42 details:

1. You begin in a neutral position
2. You drop your head
3. Your left hand reaches for the deodorant
4. Your left hand lifts the deodorant
5. Your right hand twists the cap counter-clockwise
6. Your right hand places the cap on the counter
7. Your right arm drops to the side
8. You lift your head
9. Your right arm moves straight up
10. You show disgust on your face
11. You move your face to the left
12. Your left hand places the deodorant under your armpit
13. Your left hand rubs the deodorant under your right armpit
14. Your left arm swings back to the left side
15. Your right arm "fans" your armpit
16. Your right arm drops to the side
17. Your head moves to the center position
18. Your right hand takes the deodorant from your left hand
19. Your right arm swings back to the right side
20. Your left arm moves straight up
21. You show disgust on your face
22. You move your face to the right side
23. Your right hand positions the deodorant under your left armpit
24. Your right arm rubs the deodorant under your left armpit
25. Your right arm swings back to the right side
26. Your left arm fans your armpit
27. Your left arm drops to the side
28. Your head moves to the center position
29. Your left hand takes deodorant from right hand and swings back to the left
30. You drop your head
31. Your right hand picks up the cap
32. Your right hand swings to the left, twists the cap

back on, clockwise
33. Your right arm drops to the side
34. Your left hand puts the deodorant down
35. Your left arm drops to the side
36. Your right arm moves straight up
37. Your face, positioned under your right armpit, sniffs
38. Your face moves back to center, expressing happiness
39. Your left arm moves straight up
40. Your face, positioned under your left armpit, sniffs
41. Your face moves back to center, expressing happiness
42. You extend both arms out and smile

This pantomime exercise encourages students to place energy and emphasis on single actions, and I want to make sure their actions are clear and precise when they perform them. Exercises, such as this one, pay dividends later on, when students perform scene work or participate in plays, where they want their work to be especially exact and under control, exercising, at all times, discipline of movement and complete focus, committed to being in the moment.

VOCAL/VERBAL WARM-UPS

16. Sound-and-Movement Mimic

This one is a standard sound and movement exercise. I assemble the students in a large circle. I tell them I will make a simple sound with a corresponding movement. When I finish, I will freeze. I want them to repeat exactly what I do. It's important that the sound and movement have energy and clarity. The movement should utilize the whole body, not just an arm or hand. I show the students the difference between an emphatic movement and a lazy, uninteresting movement. I want to condition them to use their entire body. It will pay dividends as the year progresses. I give an example, creating a movement utilizing my whole body: legs, back, arms, neck, backside, feet. I tilt, bend, and stretch. The sound I make is a single, sustained sound, but it is alive with energy and communication. It is presented to my audience, not kept inside. After I demonstrate my sound and movement, I freeze. The students copy me. They effectively use their bodies and their voices in a dramatic, communicative way. I do another sound and movement. They copy again. I do maybe ten of these, all different, of course. I recommend that you, the teacher/director, lead this exercise to show students effective examples of sound and movement. Later, when students become more able and confident, have them become the leaders of this exercise. I will have them perform one at a time, around the circle, and the rest of the class will copy. I don't use this format in the beginning, however. The reason is simple: students may not provide proper examples for each other. Start by showing them the standard. If they don't see and do the standard, they will not learn it. I can't write this enough times: effectively model what you want your students to perform.

17. Repeats

I call this exercise "Repeats," and it's a staple of my drama class. It's a combination of verbal, nonverbal and vocal repeats. It's very simple: whatever I say or do, the students "repeat." While it's similar to sound and movement repeats, it's much more focused on verbal language. At the start of the year, I'll use this exercise as a way to review names. I'll point out Dave, for instance, and play around with his name, while, of course, pointing him out. I might have fun with the initial consonant sound, saying, DDDDDDDDDDDD...ave. And the class will repeat. I'll emphasize the D sound, sometimes fast, sometimes slow.

I can do the same thing with any name: Mary, emphasizing the M, or Tom, emphasizing the T. It's a great way to review names while having fun with letters and sounds. I want my students to know right from the start that letters and sounds have energy, that there's a power and passion in any letter.

Speaking of letters, I often do this repeat exercise with the alphabet. Just start with the letter A: stretch it out, use it in different tones, in different pitches; explore its many possibilities. Sometimes I create sounds that are akin to alphabet sounds but not quite the same. Again, I rely on my imagination and the magic of the moment. It's important that I have fun. If the students see me relaxed and enjoying myself, they will follow suit, and everyone in the room will be unified and in sync.

Of course, I can use words and sentences with the repeats. Take the words "Holy Moly." I can use these two words and get quite a bit of mileage out of them, just with the possibility of sounds, emphasis and repetition. "Holy holy holy holy Moly Moly Moly." I can add character voices. Again, I don't think about what I'm going to do. I just do it. And this is an important lesson for the students. I always tell them, Don't think, just do. Thinking blocks, Doing frees. Play with sounds and words, and I guarantee your students will be absolutely engaged, while learning to accent syllables, vowels and consonants. Choose similar sounding words or alliterations: "Hippity Hippitty Hop Hop Hop. Hoppity Hoppity Hip Hip Hip." The variation for sound play is limitless here, adding, whenever I please, varying tones, pitches and rates. "Repeats" lays some of the most important foundational work I do in my drama class. It's a great way to model effective pronunciation, articulation and an overall reverence for sounds and words. And, best of all, it's not something I have to plan. I open my mouth and speak playfully and dramatically, opening the doors for the students' expressions.

18. Aah-Eeh-Ooh

Related to "Repeats," I call this one the "aah-eeh-ooh" exercise. Primarily a vocal warm up, it can be used anytime. First I have the students explore the "aah" sound. After I have them breathe in, I conduct with my arms, signaling them how I want them to exhale the sound. If I want them to build, to crescendo, I will raise my arms up. If I want them to decrescendo, I move my arms down. They manipulate the sound "aah," traveling up and down with it, sustaining it, until I cut them off, abruptly, using my arms as a signal to stop. I expect my students to stop at the same moment, and when they do, we achieve—as much as it's humanly possible to achieve—perfection. I have everyone listen to the silence, because silence is perfect, I often say. I am, of course, laying the foundation for something that will be addressed later in the class: the beauty of a pause.

I do the same with the "eeh" and "ooh" sounds. Then I combine all three sounds, so that we move from one to the next with the same breath. At any time I might cut them off. It's a sound exercise, a visual exercise (they have to watch me) and a silence exercise.

19. Jack and Jill Repeat

I am partial to using nursery rhymes during "Repeats." Here's one that my students particularly enjoy: I use the Jack and Jill story, adding consonants and rhythm. It's something that must be seen and heard to fully appreciate. Still, I'll try to explain it as best I can. The letters indicated in parenthesis get sounded out:

Jack (kk) and Jill (ll) went up (pp) the hill (ll) to fetch (ch, ch) a pail (ll) of water, water, water, water, water.

I vary the ending by repeating the word "water" five times. Sometimes I substitute the added consonants for two claps: Jack (clap, clap) and Jill (clap, clap) went up (clap, clap) the hill (clap, clap) to fetch (clap, clap) a pail (clap, clap) of water, water, water, water, water.

20. Whether the Weather is Cold

I use another rhyme, one I borrowed and modified from an exercise I did in college many years ago. I have students repeat these lines slowly, at first, in five parts:

> *Whether the weather is cold,*
> *Or whether the weather is hot,*
> *We'll be together,*
> *Whatever the weather,*
> *Whether we like it or not.*

When I speak these words and lines, I stretch out each sound emphatically, syllable by syllable, striking each consonant and stretching the vowels. When the students have the words and lines memorized, I have them repeat them five or six times, carefully. Then I'll play around with different tones, different rates and pitches. I usually add movements to the different emotions. If they repeat it happily I'll have them use appropriate gestures and movements, the same with angry or any emotion. It's fun to play around with speed as well. Start slowly and increase the speed, or start fast and slowly decrease the speed. Start with a low pitch and increasingly speak with a higher pitch. Often I divide the class into five different groups, each receiving a section. I assign contrasting tones to each group. For example, one group speaks the first part angrily; the next group speaks its part innocently; the next group sings its lines, and so forth. What I'm communicating here with this exercise—and in any repeat exercise—is that the speaking of language is joyful, playful and exhilarating. This exercise can take anywhere from 5-15 minutes, depending on how many variations I use and how much the students are enjoying the activity.

21. Alphabet Repeats

This exercise uses what's required to form alphabet sounds. I get students to concentrate on their mouths, tongues, lips, palates and jaws in order to articulate properly. I sound out the alphabet letter A, stretching my mouth and lips. The students mimic me. I sound out the letter B. The students do the same. I ask them the difference between forming an A sound and a B sound. They notice in the A position the lips part and the mouth stretches. In the B position, the lips join. I have them pronounce the letter C. They are aware of their tongues on the back of their teeth. When they repeat the D sound, they notice how the tongue touches lightly on the palate. They are aware that creating the E sound is similar to creating the A sound. When they make the F sound, their top teeth touch their lower lip. I continue this exercise with the rest of the alphabet.

While this exercise may not be as invigorating and imaginative to the students, they understand that proper sounds are not produced automatically. Speaking requires effort, energy and correct technique, using the mouth, tongue, jaw, lips, and palate. I have the students repeat A, very slowly, five times, to feel the energy, as well as the position, of the A sound. And then they do the same for B, C, D, E, and F. Each of these sounds is a wonder. A sound can be exciting, and in drama class they must be exciting. I can't emphasize enough how important this exercise is to the foundational work of the class. The focus on sounds, the appreciation of sounds, the sounding out of sounds, the beauty of sounds, and what it takes to form these sounds properly. Alphabet repeats is something I use all the time. In fact, it is one of the staple exercises for my cast when we're rehearsing and warming up before performances. I never assume my students are ready to speak. Therefore, I give them exercises to ensure they're ready.

22. Number Repeats

This exercise is another wonderful and effective vocal tool, which forces students to open their mouths and accentuate sounds properly. Count to ten slowly, each number five times, to become conscious of the mechanical position in the mouth for each number and what's required to produce sounds effectively, clearly and energetically. Students must be conditioned to open their mouths, and that's what "Repeats" helps accomplish. Most of my students have developed bad habits before taking my class. Specifically, they are used to mumbling (talking) instead of speaking. So, right from the beginning, I must break this bad habit. I must emphasize the difference between talking and speaking. Talking, I tell them, can be produced lazily. Speaking, however, requires effort, a conscientiousness of sounds and positions in the mouth, an attitude of motivation and aggressiveness. Therefore, I eliminate the word "talking" from my drama vocabulary. I use the word "speaking" instead because speaking is a communication skill, and that's what I want them to focus on when they open their mouth: communicating to an audience (each other). These foundational exercises (these repeats), if used diligently and repetitively, will bring the desired results: improved speaking skills for all students.

23. One Fine Day in the Month of May

"Repeats" is one of the staple exercises I use. Nearly every day I make up a rhyme that I can use in my class for vocal and articulation warm ups. This one is yet another rhyme repeat I use:

> *One fine day in the month of May, I was walking down the street with my friend named Ray.*

I say this sentence slowly, stretching the sounds, accentuating them. I have the students repeat the sentence the same way I say it. Then I play with it, and when I say play with it, I mean there are literally hundreds of ways to play with sounds and words. For instance, I might say, "*One FINE FINE day in the MONTH MONTH MONTH MONTH MONTH of May, I was WALKING WALKING*

WALKING with my friend named Ray." I vary how many times I say a word. I vary how fast or slow I speak. I vary my tone. I vary my pitch. I vary my character voice. What's important is that I speak well, model good language and speaking skills. I enjoy speaking words, enjoy playing with sounds, and if I enjoy myself—engaged in the speaking of language—the students will follow suit. I enjoy "Repeats," as much as any exercise for it's really a celebration of sounds, words, sentences and rhythms. If I succeed in conveying the excitement of communicating language, the students will develop positive associations and begin learning without knowing they're learning. My main objective has always been the following: make my students enjoy themselves so much they don't know they're learning.

24. Shake it out

After a movement exercise such as the previous one, I'll have the students disengage and shake out their hands. I like to use a vocal, along with this physical action. I say, "Shake it out, shake it out, shake, shake, shake it out." The students repeat my action and my words. I like to do this repeat fast tempo, since the students typically shake out their hands fast.

25. I Got Sand in My Pants

This one is a companion to "Shake it out." I wave my arms at my sides, in undulating movements, saying, "I got sand in the pants, I got sand in my pants, I got sand, I got sand, I got sand in my pants." I speak these words rhythmically as I coordinate them with my movements. I play with the words as I would in any "Repeat" exercise.

26. There Was an Old Lady...

As I've mentioned previously, I favor, in my "Repeats" to use nursery rhymes and poetry, anything that's rhythmic and musical. And, of course, I tailor everything to suit my personality. Here's another one I use:

There was an old lady who lived in a shoe.
Oh my, oh my, oh my.

Now, I can literally speak these lines dozens of ways, and I often do. Think about the possibilities. How many character voices can you create? How many different emotions can you communicate? How many ways can you change the emphasis? How many ways can you say the lines and add pauses? How can you manipulate the rate?
I can teach so many important voice techniques just with a simple sentence. I can emphasize pronunciation, timing, tempo, or what I like to call the ebb and flow of speaking, the rise and fall.

27. Tiger, Tiger

Here's one I use, from a famous William Blake poem:

Tiger, tiger, burning bright,
in the forests of the night.

I speak it five times, each time faster, more dramatic and intense. I speak it in multiple emotions, emphasizing different words. I speak it one syllable at a time, adding an action with each syllable, to encourage students to understand the connection between words and actions. Everything I say and do, they say and do. It's simple, yet very effective.

28. Repeats with Vowel Rhymes

I take a simple sentence such as, "I once had a father named Joe" and fill in the blank with as many rhymes as I can. For instance, "I once had a father named Joe, he lived on a boat in Tokyo." "I once had a father named Joe, his favorite author was Edgar Allen Poe." "I once had a father named Joe, he played the flute and guitar, not the oboe." "I once had a father named Joe, he rode to New York on a buffalo." I have the students repeat each of these rhymes.

Sometimes I say the first part of the sentence and tell the students to fill in the blank. I say "I once had a father named Joe..." Someone in the circle says "On Christmas morning he shouts "Ho Ho Ho." I do this exercise with all the vowels. "I once had a sister Marie; every time I saw her she was climbing a tree." "I once had a brother named Guy, he wore waxed wings, thought he could fly." "I once had a brother named Ray, he talked in his sleep, said hey, hey, hey." "I once had a mother named Sue, there wasn't any task she couldn't do." I'll say the first part of the sentence, and go around the circle, having students fill in the rhymes. If someone can't think of a rhyme, it's not a problem. The next student in the circle will jump in and finish the sentence. It's an engaging and challenging activity, to see how far the group can continue with the same vowel or rhyme.

29. Control, Discipline, Focus, Concentration

Sometimes I have students repeat important words and concepts, related to drama, such as the following:

Control. Discipline. Focus. Concentration.

I have them repeat these words ten times. I want them to hear these words in their ears, feel them on their lips, consume them in their minds. I want them to know, every day, in every exercise, that these words and concepts are the driving force behind everything we do. They are the foundation of our house. Without them, the house comes tumbling down. Every activity requires control. At all times, they must exercise discipline. Without the ability to focus and concentrate, everything they do in drama has limited effect.

And, if I'm being honest, I'm not only addressing drama. While I never, at any time, confuse my class with "Life Skills 101," I know, nonetheless, that teaching drama affords me the opportunity to teach fundamental skills, for life. After all, where does anyone go without the ability to focus? Without the ability to be disciplined? Without the ability to exercise control? Without the ability to concentrate on daily tasks? I don't teach drama to high school students to train them to be actors (though some do choose this path). I want my students—all of them—to develop skills that will help them with whatever endeavors they choose in life.

Of course, while I mention words such as control, discipline, focus and concentration all the time, they are generally masked by exercises that stimulate the students' imaginations and playful spirits. And this, I suppose, is the key to all teaching: to make the students learn in a context where they are not conscious that they are being taught.

30. Pronunciation Drill

Every time students open their mouths it should be with the purpose of being clear and exact. To meet this end, I often use words that are similar in sound, but very different, such as "lightning" and "lighting." If a student is not mechanically proficient, he may pronounce one when he means the other. Therefore, a large part of training my students to articulate is making them conscious of what they're doing, knowing where they are, and being motivated to communicate. Otherwise it's very easy for them, or anyone, including me, to be lazy in speech.

I like to use the following example, using my best New York accent: I say, "Jeet Jet?" Students typically look at me, with dumbfounded expressions. I ask them to tell me what I'm saying. I say it again, "Jeet Jet?" In all my years of giving this example, I can't remember more than a few students— out of more than a thousand—who were able to guess what I was saying. The reason no one knows what I'm saying is that I am not communicating clearly. I am not moving my mouth or jaw or using my tongue or striking the alphabet letters and syllables properly. I say it again, this time striking my consonants, stretching my vowels, opening my mouth, with the intent to be precise and clear. With the proper motivation and mechanical execution, I am able to say, "Did you eat yet?" instead of "Jeet Jet?" I recommend you try this example with your students, even if you don't have my New York accent.

Here are some common sounding words, which I borrowed from somewhere long ago, that can cause confusion. It's a good idea to sound out each word several times, slowly, accentuating the proper syllables and consonants:

1. Feet, fee, feed, feel, feels
2. Shoot, chew, choose, chewed
3. Hoot, hoof, whose, hooves
4. Wit, wish, witch, wished
5. Caught, called, coarse, cause, caused, call
6. Back, bag, backed, bang, banged
7. Right, rice, rind, rhyme

This list provides a small example of words with similar sounds. I'm sure you can develop this exercise further. The point is that students improve through repetition, and this is the reason that "Repeats" and verbal pronunciation work should be done every day. Almost daily, I bring to the class lines from poems or stories or plays. Shakespeare, of course, provides a seemingly endless array of lines that are appropriate and engaging for vocal and pronunciation work. I use this appropriate line from Hamlet: "Speak the speech I pray you, as I pronounced it to you, trippingly on the tongue." I always bring in lines from great poems: "Do not go gentle into that good night. Old age should burn and rave at close of day; rage, rage against the dying of the light." "Pity me not because the light of day at close of day no longer walks the sky."

As often as possible, I model my love of language and words for my students. While I use this language to help my students develop proper speech, I'm also conveying the inherent beauty of literature. I want them to know great language. I want them to speak it. Of course, what they repeat and speak doesn't have to be great literature. I also like to speak old ditties, things I remember as a child: "Charlie says, I love my good and plenty. Charlie says, I really love it swell. Charlie says, I love my good and plenty. I don't know any other candy that I love so well." You probably don't know this one unless you were born before

1955. Here's another one: "Don't walk in the middle, in the middle, in the middle, in the middle, in the middle, in the middle, in the middle, of the block. Look both ways before you cross the street."

Using alliteration and assonance is also highly recommended for vocal and repetitive work:

1. Snip, snap, snoop, snip
2. Bitter batter better butter
3. Kit, kat, kite, kool, kate
4. Strike, struck, strung, string
5. Wheeze, sneeze, breeze, fleas
6. Feet, feed, fee, feel, feeble

It's not that significant from where you get your words and lines. What's important is the concentration on getting students to open their mouths and speak with an energy and clarity that is not normally associated with their everyday talking.

31. Sentence Changes

Here is another "Repeat" exercise, with more input from the students. The group stands in a large circle. I speak a sentence. This sentence gets passed around the circle, perhaps five or six times. Each student will speak the sentence in his own unique way. I give an example before we begin. I say, "Many, many years ago in a far away place, I met a man who had no face." When I say this sentence the first time, I pause after the word "man" to add emphasis to the fact that he had no face. The next time I say the sentence I stress the word "met" because it's the key verb of the sentence, and verbs are the engines of sentences. They drive the thought. I want students to know the importance of verbs.

In my following example, I emphasize "far away place." Lastly, I pause after the words "years ago" to add emphasis to "in a far away place". Doing this exercise is a good way for students to learn that meaning is flexible, determined by tone, emphasis and a well-placed pause. I say another sentence: "I can't believe she didn't call me to give me to give me the news about her wedding plans." Everyone repeats. The student to my right speaks next. He says the same sentence, changing it. The class repeats. I go around the circle five times with this sentence. It's interesting how students contrast each other in tone, pitch, rate, etc. After five times, I speak a new sentence, and we continue where we left off in the circle. I always go completely around the circle, to ensure that every student gets a chance to speak and change a sentence.

32. Projection Practice using Poetry Lines

I give everyone in the circle a slip of paper. On the paper is a sentence, a line of poetry. Here are some examples of poetry lines I give my students:

> *Death closes all; but something ere the end, some work of noble note may yet be done, not unbecoming men that strove with Gods.*

> *The lights begin to twinkle from the rocks; the long day wanes; the slow moon climbs; the deep moans round with many voices.*

> *Pity me not because the light of day at close of day no longer walks the sky.*

> *Oh, methinks how slow this old moon wanes.*

> *Awake the pert and nimble spirit of mirth.*

> *Bring out the death ship, for the flood is upon us.*

> *O, thou Lord of Life, send my roots rain.*

> *Oh, how full of scorpions is my mind, dear wife.*

> *I speak of old stones that gather in the drift, in the rising tides falling by the shore.*

O, my beautiful one, can you hear the rushing wind from whence the cutting arrow comes?

I direct my students to walk in the circle, sound out the words given to them, and memorize the words. After a couple of minutes, I have them walk around and share their line of poetry with five other students. Afterwards, I split the class into two groups. Half of them go to the back of the theater and sit in the last row. The other half stays on stage. These students make a straight horizontal line, facing the audience in the last row. I tell them they're task is to communicate their line clearly, slowly, one sound and one syllable at a time, and to project their voices so they can be heard comfortably in the back of the theater. Before they speak their lines individually, I direct them in a vocal exercise. I have them breathe in and ask them to keep their eyes on the back of the theater, to where there is a glass light booth above where the students in the back are sitting. I tell them to breathe in and visualize their breath and air reaching the glass booth. I have them yawn and allow the air to travel and sustain, ten seconds. I instruct them to place their hands on their chests and diaphragms, to breathe and sound out "AAA", "OOO" and "EEE", to feel the vibration, and, as well, a relaxation. After they finish their vocal warm ups, I instruct the students to practice for a few minutes, while I go to the back of theater to speak with my other students because they have a job as well. They are the audience, and this means they need to know how to be an audience.

I haven't discussed this part of my class yet. Let me say that, for me, this element is as important as any other. I can never mistakenly assume my students know how to be an audience. I must emphasize—and keep reinforcing this point—the role of the audience. I tell them that their job is as important as those on stage. They must receive the communication. If they're not attentive and receptive, there is no communication. They must help the person on stage by providing support and encouragement. The performer and audience are in collusion. They need each other. Therefore, the bottom line is this: the audience must listen, attentively, and respond appropriately. Talking or reacting inappropriately is not part of the audience job description. If someone in the audience fails to uphold the standard that is required, I must stop immediately and rectify the problem. This is an area of my class where I cannot compromise my standards. If it requires me to follow up many times, then that's what I'll do, until the class—as a whole—satisfies the proper requirements of an ideal audience.

Now, back to the exercise on stage. One at a time, the students speak their line of poetry. But there are rules: They must stretch their vowels, accentuate their consonants, speak slowly sound by sound, syllable by syllable—and, of course, they must project in a relaxed way. I do not want them to shout. In fact, I demonstrate the difference between speaking/projecting in a relaxed way and shouting. Shouting requires too much effort and will ruin their voices. If they breathe correctly, concentrate on relaxing and controlling their breath and air, and if they visualize the movement of the sound, they will succeed. I know this is easier said than done, but with practice and concentrated effort and motivation, they will definitely improve and, thus, succeed.

The students sitting in the back—as part of their requirement—must listen and receive the sound, the clarity of the lines. When each student finishes on stage, I want the group in the back to clap if they hear the sounds comfortably, and if they understand the words clearly. If they don't clap, the student on stage should give it another try. This exercise is not meant to criticize anyone. Its intent is to guide the students, give them feedback, to help them understand the difference between acceptable stage sound and ineffective sound. Remember, this is foundational work. If someone on stage is mumbling, I stop him, and review the standards of speaking and projecting. If necessary, I model for the student and have him mimic me. Whatever it takes to get the student to stretch and learn, I do. Often, what it takes is energy: follow through, a commitment to what I'm teaching, a determination to succeed at teaching. I don't want to cheat myself, and I especially don't want to cheat my student.

If the students pass these early tests, they will relax and become loose, and perform with confidence—with their natural genius—the rest of the year. It's a very exciting process, but the basic work must be done early. Believe me, the students appreciate the feedback. Besides, the majority of students have great success with this exercise. It empowers them to know they are in control of their speaking destiny. When the first group finishes, I have the other group come up on stage and follow the same procedure as before.

I recommend you gather great lines of poetry. I have hundreds I've collected over the years. They're great for repeats, for any language work, and especially for this exercise I just described. Getting the students to speak clearly and project their voices is not an easy task, not for any of us involved. You can turn it into something beautiful, though, by including the language of the poets.

On another note: I've written the word "confidence" many times in this book, and I don't mean to imply that confidence is something easily conjured or manufactured. It's not. Students (all of us) need to earn confidence. I see students develop confidence all the time, and it's the most satisfying part of my job. I also know where that confidence comes from. It comes from effort and motivation, from taking risks, from stepping beyond the threshold of fear, into the light of freedom and expression. These exercises, all of them, collectively, help the students find that light. I can't lie. I don't see it in the first 30 days. But I guarantee these exercises are the foundation for that confidence, and it does become evident down the road, sometime during the "beyond" part of the class. It all starts here, however, with practice, with foundational work.

FOCUS WARM-UPS

33. Two-Person Mirror

I use many variations of the mirror exercise, as I will be pointing out in subsequent exercises. The first one I use involves two students facing each other, perhaps three feet apart. I have three specific requirements for this exercise. Here's what I want them to do:

- Maintain a neutral expression. Students cannot smile, laugh, contort or move their faces.
- Keep eyes on eyes. Students cannot look down, up or away.
- Place palms and hands out, mirroring the other student's palms and hands.

One of the students leads, moving his hands slowly. The slower the better. These three requirements must be evident to have a successful mirror exercise. Before I divide the class into pairs, I have two assistants demonstrate for the class. I have the class make a small circle around the two students who are demonstrating. As they begin the exercise, I point out to the class what they're doing. "Notice their eyes," I say. "Notice how neither one is moving his eyes. Also notice how each keeps a neutral expression. Neither one of them is expressing any emotion, no smiles, no frowns, just neutral. Also notice the slow the movements of the hands. They are barely moving. The slower the better, because it reflects greater control, more focus and concentration."

The first time they do it, I have the students mirror each other for 30 seconds. I walk around and observe, commending the ones who successfully align the three required elements, and giving specific feedback to those who don't succeed. Perhaps their eyes are moving or they don't keep a neutral expression. I tell them what they must fix and have them try it again. I don't settle for 80% class success. I make sure everyone succeeds, no matter how many times he has to repeat it. The two-person mirror is not something I have my students do once and forget about. It is foundational. The more proficient the students become, the more they want to do it. Focus is addictive. Students feel in control, empowered. The mirror is a simple exercise, but it can have profound effects on the students.

34. Mirror Using Parallel Lines

I create two lines, facing each other, about fifteen feet apart. Students must mirror the student across from them. The guidelines are the same as the two-person mirror, with a couple of variations. I tell one line of students they will be the leaders. At some point I say, "freeze," then "switch." At that time, the other line of students becomes the leaders. I say "switch" every 15 seconds. This format really forces the students to concentrate on their partner, since they can see many students in the line. This one challenges the students more, since it includes directions and more possible distractions.

35. Mirror Using Parallel Lines and Directions

This mirror exercise is an extension of the previous one. I keep the students in their same lines. This time I tell them that I'm going to give directions to one of the lines. All the students in this line must move according to my direction. The students in the opposite line then mirror the first line. The tricky part is that the students doing the mirror must use opposite actions. For instance, I'll tell the first line: "Raise your right arm." The students opposite them, in order to mirror correctly, must raise their left arm. If I say "Take one step forward with your right leg" the students opposite must take one step forward with their left leg. If I say "Move your head to the right" the students opposite must move their heads to the left. It's a good idea, at some point, to change the leaders, so that all the students get a chance taking directions and mirroring, using opposite actions. While this one may be classified more as a game than a mirror exercise, it is, nonetheless a worthwhile activity, for it not only tests the students listening and direction-taking skills, but it challenges their reflexes and timing reactions.

36. Mirror With Four Leaders

I now introduce a group mirror exercise. I call this one "Four leaders." I pick four students from the large circle and have them stand in the inner circle. I instruct them to stand and face in four different directions: North, West, South and East. The rest of the students in the circle are already in an area (north, west, south or east). Each of the students in the middle strikes a pose. For this mirror exercise the rules change a little. The students in the middle, the leaders, still assume a neutral expression.

However, they look straight ahead, not directly at the students in the circle. The students in the circle, however, look specifically at their leader, at his eyes. Here's another difference: the leader is not restricted to slow hand movements. He still must move very slowly, but he can use his entire body; he may move his leg up or down or forward or back; he may tilt his body. In other words, more freedom of movement is allowed to the leaders. I tell the leaders to keep it simple, however. The object is for the students in the circle to follow their leader. So what's happening in this exercise is that there are four different groups, each one doing something entirely different. I have students perform this exercise for several minutes, maybe longer.

Of all the mirror exercises I use, this one is my favorite because it's fascinating to watch four entirely different groups, moving in their own way, meanwhile conforming to the rules of the Group Soul: everyone unified, in sync with one another, in the same place, at the same time, a moving picture of collective focus. Few moments in my drama class exist that are as satisfying as this one when it is performed according to the directions.

37. You Can't Break My Focus

What I just referred to is a perfect segue into the next exercise. I call this one, "You can't break my focus." The object for each student, no matter the distraction, is to keep his focus. I set out five chairs, facing the audience. I tell the students that everyone is going to have his or her chance to sit on one of the chairs. I explain the exercise. It's as important as any exercise we do all year. I have an advanced student demonstrate. The student sits in the chair, faces the class. The student sits upright, not slouched, head up, eyes straight ahead. It's very important that the eyes stay open, and it's equally important that the student keep a neutral expression throughout. That's it. Neutral expression, eyes open, head straight. Then I send up 4-5 students, whom I call distractors. These students try to break the student's focus.

Here are the rules for the distractors: they must stand behind or to the side of the student who's sitting; they cannot touch the student; they can talk, whisper, make crazy sounds, do whatever it takes to break the student's concentration. I purposely start with one of my advanced students because I know he will keep his focus. He will provide the example I want my class to see. Once the other students see this student succeed, they understand what they must do. The objective for the students sitting down is to keep their focus for one minute. If they last one minute, they achieve elite concentration status. This exercise is exciting for the students to watch, and it's challenging for the students sitting down. It does take time, perhaps 25-30 minutes, depending on how many students I have in my class. I take my time, however, because I need to know who can focus—who's ready to do drama—and who needs further conditioning and strengthening of their skills.

38. Large Group Mirror

For this mirror exercise I have my students stand in a large circle. Each student looks straight ahead, focusing his eyes on an object, not on another student. He keeps a neutral expression. I choose one student to be the leader. He moves his hands and arms into a position, the same way someone in "Four Leaders" does. He begins moving slowly.

The rest of the students in the circle mirror him, without looking at him. It's important that their eyes do not move. They should be locked in one place, and their faces should remain neutral.

These are the most important requirements. If their hand movements aren't exactly the same, that's okay. But the eyes and facial expressions must be solidly in place. At some point, I say, "Freeze" and switch the leader. The new student takes over, and everyone follows him. I usually switch the leader every thirty seconds. I do this activity for several minutes.

39. Small Group Mirror

For this one I divide the large group into smaller units, usually six in a group. I have each group form a small circle. The small group can do the same mirror exercise as I just described. Each group chooses a leader. Everyone is looking straight ahead, with a neutral expression, eyes locked in place. Many variations exist for the small group mirror exercise. I can have the students, on their own, switch the leaders, or I may call out "freeze" and "switch."

Another variation is having the students hold their arms and hands up. They connect their hands and move slowly, while their eyes are locked, and they keep their neutral expressions. Whatever I choose, I must make sure the mirror activity remains a focus exercise. If their eyes are moving, they're not focusing. If they're smiling, they're not focusing. It's important that I walk around. If they're not doing it correctly, I have them start again. I have them keep doing it until they get it right; otherwise it's a wasted activity.

40. Neutral Position Breathing

As I listed earlier, breathing exercises are also an important element of my daily regime of activities. Breathing exercises train students to focus and slow down, to be in the moment. The first one I do is simple. I say the following: "Stand in a neutral position, place your arms at your sides, stand straight, feet slightly apart, relax your shoulders, look straight ahead, lock your eyes in place, and keep a neutral expression. Now, inhale a deep breath, feel your diaphragm expand, hold your breath, now exhale." I have them repeat this breathing pattern three times. They typically exhale with silent breath, though sometimes I have them breath in, hold, and then "sigh" out the breath. This exercise can be done with eyes open or closed.

41. Breathing, Adding Arms

I often add arm movements to the breathing. I have students raise their arms from their sides as they breath in to simulate the intake of breath. I show them. I stand in neutral position. I lock my eyes, on a spot on the stage (I prefer looking down rather than up.) I breathe in slowly and as I do, my arms raise slowly as well, just at my sides. I hold my breath, stop my arms. As I exhale, my arms slowly go back to their resting place at my side. This last move I can do this with palms up or palms down. It's very important that the arm movements and the exhalation of breath are slow and controlled. I have my students breathe this way three times. I watch their eyes, making sure they are locked in one place, not moving around. I watch to make sure their inhalation and exhalation are slow, that their arms movements coordinate with their breath.

42. Breathing with Sway

This is one of my favorite breathing exercises. The first time I introduce it, I demonstrate for the class. I stand in a neutral position, my arms at my side. I lock my eyes on a spot on stage. When I breathe in, I sway my body forward, just slightly. I don't want to lose my balance. When I exhale, I sway back to my resting position. I add a pause before I exhale. I don't want to swing like a pendulum. I want to breathe and sway in a slow, controlled way. When the group does it—and I always do it with them— I do not give directions or speak. The moment speaks for itself: everyone's eyes locked in place; everyone breathing in and out, swaying forward and back. Though each of us has our eyes on the stage, we can, with our peripheral vision, see each other, and, believe me, when you have 36 people in a circle, breathing in and out, swaying forward and back, in perfect coordination, it's poetry in motion. It's spiritual. It personifies the Group Soul.

43. Breathing with Energy Squeeze

For this exercise, students stand in a neutral position, join hands and close their eyes. I direct them. I tell them to breathe in and gentle squeeze hands with the people nearest them on their left and right. I tell them to hold the breath and the squeeze. Then I tell them to exhale and relax their squeeze, but not to disengage their hands. I have them do it five times: breathe in, squeeze, hold, exhale and relax.

44. Dissolve, Drain and Renew

Here's another breathing/focus/relaxation exercise I do, usually once a week, on Mondays (because Mondays are hard, for everyone). I call it "Dissolve, Drain and Renew." It's a variation of what some people might call "Raggedy Ann." I demonstrate. I stand in a neutral position and close my eyes. I dissolve slowly. My head drops first. Then my upper back and lower back, vertebrae by vertebrae. I slowly bend, and as I do, my arms drop as well. My head, my torso, my midsection, continue to fall; I bend my knees, as if I'm touching my toes. I take my time. When I have dropped as far as I can, I hang there, for ten seconds or longer. I want the tiredness in me—or the stress, if that's what it is—to drain out. When I'm ready to return, renewed, I begin my ascent, reversing my movements, slowly coming back to my standing, neutral, position. I open my eyes again.

While this exercise has obvious relaxation and renewal purposes, it is fundamentally a focus and control exercise. In fact, if it's not done under control, if it's done too quickly, it will not have the desired result. Therefore, it's extremely important to model this one well. And it's equally important to observe the students carefully when they do it. Make sure their eyes remained closed, that they're not looking around them to see if others look as silly as them. Make sure they take their time. I tell them it should take, at the minimum, one minute to perform this exercise. I've had students do it for as long as five minutes. The slower—the more concentrated and controlled—the better.

45. Guess the Mirror Exercise Leader

Here's a game I play with a group mirror exercise. I had mentioned the mirror exercise in a large circle, where there is a leader and everyone else follows, without looking at the leader. I also do this variation: I send one student out of the room before the class begins. Before he leaves, I tell him his challenge, when he returns, is to guess the leader of the mirror exercise. He leaves, and I choose a leader. I must remind the students to keep their eyes locked on one spot, not on the leader. They must rely on their peripheral vision to mirror the leader's movements. They begin the mirror exercise. After 30 seconds, I have the student return to the stage. I give the student three guesses to determine the leader.

46. Guess the Changing Statues

Here's another guessing game, using the large group. This one involves poses/freezes, and it's similar to the transformation exercise. Everyone in the circle, except one student, strikes a pose (anything he wants, as long as he's using his entire body). The student who is not in the circle is given a minute to study the poses. I tell him that when he leaves the room, I will choose five students who will change their poses. Their changes should be dramatically different, The student leaves. I choose five students who change. The other students make the same exact poses as earlier. The student comes in, looks around. I give him three guesses to determine the five students who changed.

47. Eight Movements, using Mirror and Repeats

Sometimes I'll combine mirror activities with words and actions. For instance, I stand in a neutral position and slowly raise my right arm in front of me, about chest high, palms up. I do the same with my left arm, as if I'm reaching out for something. I say the words, "Come, give me your hands." I slowly close both of my hands. My right arm goes back to its resting place, and when it does, I open my hand again and relax it. I then do the same with my left arm and hand. Altogether I have eight actions, including the words I speak. I call this exercise 8 Movements. Sometimes it's 10 or 12 movements. I assign each action or words a number.

As I call out the number, the students do the action or say the words. For example, with the above example, as I say "One" they raise their right arm up. Meanwhile their eyes remain locked the entire time, their heads straight and still. When I say "Two" their left arm goes up. When I say "Three" they say the words "Come, give me your hand." When I say "Four" they slowly squeeze their hands shut. When I say "Five" they lower their right arm, relax it against their side. On "Six" they open their right hand. On "Seven" they lower their left arm, relax it against their side. Finally, on "Eight" they open their right hand.

This one-detail-at-a-time exercise not only encourages focus, control and discipline, it communicates to the students the energy they possess in their bodies: the power of their arms, moving and lifting; the opening and closing of their hands; the tilt and turn of their head to the left or right. These are powerful gestures. I start with 8 movements the first day I introduce this exercise, and increase to 10 or 12 movements on subsequent days.

VERBAL/NONVERBAL EXERCISES

48. Learning Gibberish Rules

I use gibberish a great deal: in exercises, in improvisations, in rehearsals. Therefore, it's necessary for me to establish its ground rules, to ensure students grasp it correctly. I explain that gibberish is nonsensical language that must be communicated clearly. It should never be confused with mumbling. I give an example: Koo-pa-see-mo. No such word exists, and, yet, I sound the word out clearly, accentuating all the sounds. That's rule number one: I must take my time saying this nonsensical word. I must really articulate it. Now, because the word is nonsensical and therefore has no meaning, I must add two important elements: distinct tone of voice and a clear action.

For instance, if I clasp my hands near my chest, smile and say gently to the class, "Koo-pa-see-mo, maka, maka," they might understand that I'm saying, in translation, "Welcome, beautiful students" because it's the tone of my voice and my accompanying actions that are what's really communicating, not my words. (And this, after all, is the primary usefulness of gibberish.) So, let's review. Here are the three essential elements to ensure I am performing gibberish properly:

1. Clear communication of all sounds
2. Definitive tone of voice
3. Specific (readable) action

To ensure the students understand and know how to execute gibberish properly, I have them repeat me. I say, "Koo-pa-see-mo, maka, maka" slowly and clearly. I say it gently. I smile; I clasp my hands near my chest, very paternal-like. The students do the same. I give another example. I'm a little more excited for this one. I'm recalling a moment I got a big hit in a baseball game. I'm holding an imaginary baseball bat, crouched in a stance; my voice is urgent. "She-stoopa-luupa, popo." (translated: "The pitcher threw the ball.") I speak and swing the bat at the same time. "Tomminee, ballamie, crish, croom, stoko." (Translated: "I hit the ball over the second baseman's head!") I drop the bat and raise my arms over my head. "Neenamoopseepa, Neenamoopseepa!" (Translated: "We won the game, we won the game!") I have the students mimic my crystal clear gibberish, my tone and actions. I can't emphasize enough to my students how important it is to slow down when speaking gibberish. While it sounds contradictory, these nonsensical words must ring out with clarity. Treat these words, I tell them, with all the respect of the most revered words in the English language.

49. Practicing Specific Actions in Gibberish

I focus this exercise on the difference between specific and general actions. I recall the previous exercise when I was holding and swinging an imaginary baseball bat. That, I point out, is a specific (readable) action. If I tell the same baseball story minus the action of swinging the bat—if all I do is pace back and forth and wave my arms without definition—the students, or my audience, will not be able to "read" my actions.

The reason is simple: general actions do not communicate clearly. They are open to interpretation, and that is not what you want to accomplish in your gibberish exercises. So I focus the first exercise on specific actions. Let's take gardening, for instance. I ask the students to tell me the type of actions that are associated with gardening.

They respond with the following: watering plants, clipping flowers and bushes, pulling weeds, shoveling dirt. These are all specific (readable) actions. I tell the students to lift an imaginary shovel and start digging. They do. It's hard to mistake this action. I further develop the point by presenting the following gibberish example: I shovel dirt for about ten seconds, then stop and wipe my brow. I rub my lower back and say tiredly (remember, you need the emotion) "Sella, tee, bock, bock, fumastat," making sure to speak slowly and clearly. (Translation: "This work is killing my back.") I have students do the same actions, and, with the same emotion and clarity, say, "Sella, tee, bock, bock, fumastat." This practice—this repetition—conditions them to satisfy the three necessary elements of gibberish, in the recommended order: always start with the action, then add the emotion and, finally, speak the gibberish.

I continue with specific actions. I tell the students, "You are holding a hose, watering the garden." I check to make sure everyone is doing this action clearly. If the action is clear, even without comprehensible words, I already know the setting—and possibly the subject—of the story. Next I say, "You are bending down, pulling weeds." Again, I check to make sure everyone is performing this action clearly. I continue: "You have large clippers in your hands, you are trimming the roses (or any flowers)."

I recommend you spend sufficient time reviewing specific actions. Choose an activity that is familiar to them, such as Sports. Here are directions you can give specific to sports: "You are holding a racket, waiting for the ball to come to you. It does, you hit it." "You are bouncing a basketball, once, twice, three times, looking at the basket, getting ready to toss a free throw." "You are a quarterback, your hands underneath the center, barking out the signals, getting ready to receive the ball."

50. Practicing Tone in Gibberish

Once I have established what a specific (readable) action looks like, I shift my focus to the importance of tone in deciphering gibberish. I have students practice speaking the same nonsensical words in different emotions. I have them repeat what I say: "Mellameenie, mellamo, mamee, mamo." Now I have them speak the same gibberish, using the following emotions: anger, happiness, paranoia, silliness, irritation, confusion, bossiness, frustration, etc. This exercise makes evident that it's the tone of voice—not the words themselves—that communicate meaning.

51. Practicing Clarity in Gibberish

It's a fact—or arguably so—that students need to open their

mouths to produce clear sounds, to articulate decipherable words. The speaking of gibberish requires an added emphasis on enunciation and rate. Gibberish articulation takes practice. I like to make up sounds, starting with alphabet letters: Ack, Bel, Cinto, Dobbee, etc. I have students repeat these sounds, slowly, with overt attention to syllable, vowel and consonant. The more they practice speaking nonsensical words carefully and clearly, the more familiar they will become in understanding and executing gibberish properly.

52. Large Group Gibberish Translation

Now that my students have practiced the three critical areas of gibberish, they will be ready for gibberish improvisations. Part 2 of this book ("Improvisations") will list some of my favorite ones. I'd like to describe one more large group exercise I do, as a precursor to the improvisations. I have two advanced students demonstrate a Gibberish-Translation exercise. One speaks gibberish; the other translates it into English. The gibberish student appropriately leads with an action. He's holds a bowling ball, sizes up the pins, walks, and releases the ball. He looks, then pumps his fist in the air, saying, excitedly, "To, la, po, keepa, so! Sa!" The translator performs the same actions, and says, excitedly, in English, "That's my first strike ever!"

I commend the first student for his specific (readable) actions, his definitive tone, and his clear speech. I applaud the second student for his keen observation of actions, his finely tuned ear, and his clever translation. Now we're ready to go around the circle, from student to student, alternating gibberish and translation. I tell the students doing the gibberish to choose an action familiar to them, followed by an appropriate gibberish expression. In addition, I tell them to keep it simple, that a few words, a short sentence, will suffice. This exercise requires a great deal of monitoring because, as I wrote earlier, gibberish skill needs practice. Point out the ones that succeed, that satisfy the requirements, and explain why they do, or, even better, have the students explain. If you have time, have the students switch positions, so that everyone has a chance at performing gibberish as well as translating it. This feedback—these explanations—will pay dividends later on when students are able to apply their understanding and practice of gibberish in playful, engaging improvisations.

53. Learning Genre Rules

The focus now shifts to genre exercises, which are just a different means to the same end I've been aiming to accomplish in the preceding activities: the development of verbal, vocal, and nonverbal communication. When I ask my students what I mean by "genre," they invariably mention categories of movies, books, TV shows, etc. I ask them to name as many genres as they can. Together, as a class, we produce the following:

Spy thriller	Horror	Action Thriller
Mystery Thriller	Sea Adventure	Hip Hop
Opera	Cartoon	Hillbilly
Romance	Shakespeare	Fairy Tale
Country western	Foreign	Fable
Soap Opera	Detective	Tragedy
Musical Comedy	Surfer	Comedy
Children's story	Fantasy	Classical

As I have my students engage in genre activities, I use the same approach I would in gibberish, character work or just about any other exercise. I start with physical development. "Rule number one," I say. "Show the genre. If you're sitting down, show the genre. If you're standing or moving, show the genre. Each genre has a distinctive look, as well as a distinctive sound. The look precedes the words. That's the formula in drama. Show what you're going to say before you say it."

I ask questions, trying to stimulate my students' imaginations. "If you could strike one pose to represent Spy Thriller what would it be? Where are you? Who are you?

What is the situation? Is it the climactic moment? Let me see that look." I count to 3. They strike a pose. I direct them to freeze and hold for five seconds. Then I give them another genre and ask appropriate questions before having them pose and freeze. I go through 6-8 genres in this manner.

After they freeze, I instruct them to walk and, eventually, whisper a few lines, to place themselves ("whole body") in the moment they're imagining, with the help of the questions I've asked. I keep an eye and ear on them. I don't want them interacting. I want them locked into their own imaginations, believing where they are, who they are, and what is happening. I start here with genre work, naming one genre at a time, making sure to contrast them (Horror, then Cartoon, for instance) to generate as much student flexibility as possible.

54. Practicing Genres in Pairs

Here's a genre exercise that is interactive: I divide the students into pairs, and assign each pair a genre. I give each pair the same sentence to speak.

> #1: Excuse me, sir, have you seen a silly white rabbit pass by?

> #2: No, but I did see a one-legged woman tap dancing a few minutes ago.

I determine which student speaks #1 and which #2. Then I have all the #1 students repeat their line several times, to ensure they know it. I do the same with the #2 students. Before they begin performing the sentences in their assigned genres, I have them communicate their genres nonverbally (recalling the previous exercise). On the count of 3, I have all the #1 students strike a pose and freeze. I then do the same with the #2 students. Now we're ready to begin. The genres (and sentences) move around the circle, one at a time. It's always entertaining to watch and listen to this exercise, for even though the sentences spoken by each pair are the same, the scene looks and sounds different each time. That's the beauty of genres. The emphasis is not on what's being said. Rather, on how it's being said.

With these exercises the previous two days, I want to establish the creative, wide-ranging possibilities of genre play. Because they stretch students in so many beneficial ways, I return to genre exercises throughout the year, as you will discover in Sections 2-4. I use them in warm ups, in improvisations, in scene work, and, especially, in my play rehearsals. For instance, if I feel my students are thinking too much in play practice, I have them rehearse in genres. As they do their lines, I switch genres. In no time at all, students become loose and completely in the moment, and whenever that happens they make discoveries. There are few exercises I can think of that will free the students' imaginations and playful spirits the way genre activities do.

55. Techniques for Speaking Dialogue

This exercise focuses on developing techniques for working with dialogue. I arrange the chairs in a large circle and divide the class into pairs, separating them as much as I can. They're going to need room because, at times, this one involves standing or perhaps moving. I start by giving each pair the same simple, 12-line script. I purposely write a script that is vague, open to interpretation. There's a reason I don't want it to be too specific, as you will see in the various exercises I have students perform. First, here's the script:

A: Hello.
B: We finally meet.
A: Yes we do.
B: Have you considered my proposal?
A: I have.
B: And?
A: It is most generous of you.
B: Does it mean you accept the conditions?
A: Do you mind if I first ask you a question?
B: Not at all.

A: Have you ever done this before?
B: No, I have never done this before.

As you can see, this script is purposely vague and elastic. It could be about many different situations and subjects. It also can be played male/female, female/female or male/male. I use this script as a way to get students to stretch their emotional range, their speaking techniques, their outer/inner skills, and their imagination in their approach to speaking and performing language. I preface this exercise with the following comment: "All words are not created equal. Some burn like fire; some fall like dead leaves; some rest like petals in a pond." I start by having the pairs face each other. I tell them to decide who is A, who is B. I have them read the script, changing my directions as indicated below:

Direction #1: Read the script slowly, exaggerating your enunciation, speaking sound by sound, syllable by syllable, stretching the vowels, accentuating the consonants.

Direction #2: Read the script in different emotions, tones, or genres. First read it as a love scene. Next read it as a mystery. Then read it as a power struggle. (I add others as well.)

Direction #3: Read the scene with a special emphasis on the verbs

Direction #4: Read the scene with a special emphasis on the nouns.

Direction #5: Read the scene, adding large pauses anywhere you like.

Direction #6: Read the scene, starting with a whisper, slowly increasing your volume with each subsequent line.

Direction #7: Read the scene, starting with high volume, slowly decreasing to a whisper.

Direction #8: Read the scene in a low pitch, then a high pitch.

Direction #9: Read the scene, one in tears, the other chuckling. (Then switch.)

Direction #10: Read the scene, this time switching roles.

Direction #11: Read the scene in your original roles, repeating each other's lines, in different ways, before speaking your own lines.

Direction #12: Read the scene, singing the lines in a whisper.

Direction #13: Read the scene, using physical positions to influence how you speak the words (outer/inner practice).

Here are examples:

- One of you sits in the chair; the other stands and walks around, slowly circling the seated one.
- Both of you stand, back to back, as if you're glued to one another. You try to move, but you can't.
- Both of you lie on the stage, on your backs.
- One of you lies on the stage, on your back, the other crouches down.
- With your one free arm clasp the other person's arm and take turns pulling at each other when you speak your line.
- Both of you sit very straight in your chairs.
- One of you sits straight, the other slouches.
- One of you paces nervously, the other sits calmly.
- One of you is tied to the chair, the other puts one foot on the chair.
- One of you sits with your head back, yawning. The other gently raps the back of the chair as he speaks.

Depending on time and interest, I modify how many of these directions I give. Remember, everything I write here is adaptable. Choose what works for you and your students. The exercise itself, like everything I've written thus far, is one that I use periodically. I'm conditioning my students, giving them foundational work for the rest of the year. Later on, for instance, they will be performing scenes, from plays, with partners. Each time they do, I want them to experiment with their scripts in much the same way—and other ways they create on their own—that I do here. I want them to know that dialogue is elastic. It's up to them to stretch it in creative, improvisational ways. I want them to know that play is a necessary part of discovery.

56. Adding Words to Status Cards

When everyone has received a card and freezes appropriately, I choose two different looking sitting positions. I instruct these two students to engage each other in conversation, using their status, card numbers, as their influence. The other students relax during this exchange. They watch and listen. They are now the guessers. The two students interact for about one minute. Then I ask the rest of the class to guess what numbers were given to each of the speakers. I ask for at least a half dozen guesses, with appropriate explanation. It's always interesting to note the various opinions, and reasons for them. Just as with the previous exercise, I'll repeat this one four or five times.

These exercises involving the use of playing cards bring up stimulating discussions: What makes someone look or sound like a Jack? Why not a 10 or a Queen? What are the gestures we associate with a higher status or lower status? What is it about the way they walk or stand or sit? What are the specific indicators, verbal or nonverbal, that reveals status? Later on, in Section 2, I will describe some improvisations that further develop the effectiveness of using playing cards to create status and character.

57. Voice Over Pantomime using One Speaker

Here's an exercise designed to stimulate nonverbal move-ment and also develop coordination skill between speaker and actor. I direct the students to sit in chairs in the large circle. Their job is to mouth the words spoken by someone else and to move with theatrical gestures. For instance, I choose an advanced student who speaks aloud, slowly and dramatically, understanding that the rest of the students have to keep up and mouth the words as he speaks. I have him start simple, just say "Hello, everyone, how are you?" A voice over exercise is essentially a pantomime. Therefore, exaggerated body language must accompany the mouthing of words. I give this example: If I'm saying "Hello, every-one, how are you?" I must make sure I am opening my mouth in an exaggerated way. It has to appear that I am speaking the words. I might wave my arm or hand, or I might rub my hands together. Surely, my face is expressive, with excitement. I have the class mimic me as I silently say "Hello, everyone, how are you?" along with the actions I in-clude. This is not an easy exercise for students. It requires precise timing and impeccable coordination of sound and movement. To encourage the exaggerated, pantomimic element, I have the speaker continue in an exclamatory tone: "You're not going to believe what happened to me yesterday!" At this point, the students don't need to be perfect. They just need to have fun, moving their mouths, with accompanying gestures as best they can. At the very least, they are stretching their nonverbal muscles.

To help the process, I instruct the speaker to slow down as much as possible, perhaps speak one word at a time. There's another important job for the speaker. He must switch his tone continuously. If he starts off excitedly, I tell him he needs to switch to something disturbing, and then so on. If the speaker doesn't move emotionally then the voice over becomes flat and dull, monosyllabic. The voice over is akin to an emotion switching exercise.

58. Voice-Over Pantomime Changing Speakers

Here are other options I use: The class speaks and acts out one voice over sentence. Only this time the speaker changes. The student next to me on my right starts speaking. Everyone else performs the voice over. Then they continue around the circle, changing the speaker each time. Or, I might even try keeping one speaker and having the voice over change from student to student, around the circle. Or, if I have an advanced student, someone who appears to have natural instincts for voice over, I might have him perform a voice over monologue, while the speaker tells a story, changing emotions. This exercise is similar to an assignment I give students, working in pairs, later on, in which one writes a monologue, complete with shifting emotions. He practices speaking it. The other student performs the voice over. Of course, in that assignment, students will have the opportunity to practice and rehearse. Voice Over is a particularly sophisticated skill that some students naturally possess. In Section 2, I will describe the classic two-person improvisation that requires students to be lightning fast in their nonverbal reactions.

59. Outer/Inner Emotion

I call out an emotion and count to three. At the count of three, students strike a pose and freeze. If I say the word "fear," I want them to place themselves in a specific situation (an exaggerated one) where they feel fear. I tell them they must utilize their entire body, mind and spirit to convey fear completely, using the following: their faces, their eyes, their arms, their hands, their back, their legs, their feet. I ask questions: What are you thinking? Where are you? What is inside your mind? I don't want the pose to be an empty pose. I want the mind to influence the body, and the body to influence the mind. They have to work together. Just as they will later on when the students speak words from a script. The words must come from somewhere, from some drive, some motivation, some need, some purpose. Therefore, in this exercise I have them join their bodies and minds, the outer and inner. To ensure that there is a substance to their poses, I have them hold the freezes. I count out ten seconds. I tell them when I get to ten, I want them simultaneously to whisper words they are feeling, to express what's inside them. I don't want them to move. I want them to hold their poses.

This exercise has significant foundational value. Later, when students perform monologues and scripts, I have them create freezes and body positions to help them understand emotional states, to reinforce the inseparable relationship between body position and mentality. So I take the students through numerous emotions, and each time I have them freeze, hold for ten seconds, whisper for ten seconds, and then freeze again. This exercise also strengthens the control, discipline, focus and concentration muscles. They cannot interact with one another. They must focus exclusively on their own space, their own movements and feelings, not allowing themselves to become distracted.

I recommend you use contrasting emotions. For instance, if I start with fear," I will follow it up with "power" or something similarly opposite. The more you contrast emotions, the more flexible, physically and emotionally, the students will become.

60. Emotional Transformations

I call out contrasting emotions, such as fear and power, for example, or fear and confidence or excitement and fear or fear and amazement or happiness and suspicion. It's handy to have a list of contrasting emotions to which I can refer. Anyway, let's assume I am focusing on the emotion fear first. I tell students, "On the count of 3, I want you to strike a pose of fear. Use your entire body and your face." They strike their pose, and then I say, "Freeze." I tell them they are now going to transform themselves into a pose of power. I count to 10. By the time I reach 10, they should have completely transformed to power. I want them to transform slowly and systematically, not quickly.

They need to change one body part at a time. I tell them to coordinate their change to the numbers I'm counting.

For each number I count, move a specific body part. Perhaps they change their legs first, then their back, then their arms, hands, neck, head, and finally their face. This process helps them to feel the energy in different parts of their body and understand that the power of any emotion can be experienced in a hand, an arm, a back, etc. I want them to stay frozen for ten seconds. When I begin counting again I ask them to return to their fear pose, reversing their actions, one at a time. Once again, they hold for ten seconds. Then I have them "Shake it out."

This one, like most exercises should be modeled first. Students need to see the focus and control—the concentrated energy—it requires. I like to have them do four or five of these in succession. Here are some contrasting emotions that work well together:

Happy/Suspicious; Irritated/Excited; Courageous/Sick; Peaceful/Angry. This exercise trains the students to convey emotion in the body, and we know from earlier exercises how the physical can feed the emotional and verbal life.

61. Switching Emotions

This one is a variation of the walk/greet/whisper exercise I introduced on an earlier day. I walk around the circle, giving each student a different emotion. I tell the students to walk around the stage for ten seconds, expressing their emotion in movement only. Then I direct them to walk up to someone and whisper their emotion, in the proper emotion given to them, and shake hands. The other person does the same. At that point they switch emotions and walk around for ten seconds in their new emotion, until it is time to greet someone else, at which point they once again switch. The object, I tell the class, is to meet ten people and experience ten emotions.

62. Sitting Positions for Outer/Inner Emotions

I have students form a large circle, sitting in chairs. I begin by telling them to sit the exact way I sit. I slouch in my chair. They do the same. I ask, "What type of attitude does the slouching influence?" Someone says, "An I-don't-care attitude." I ask another question: "If I have an I-don't-care attitude and I'm sitting like this, what words might come out of my mouth?" A student gives an excellent example: "When is this stupid class going to be over?" "Perfect," I say. I tell the student to say the line again. He does. I tell the rest of the students, still in their slouched sitting positions, to repeat. They do.

I give another example: I lean forward and rub my hands together. My students copy this action. This position elicits a very distinct feeling in me that something important is about to happen. I say, "Wow, I can't wait to see what happens next." They continue the action and repeat the line. Now I sit tall, my back straight against the chair, my hands folded on my lap. The students sit the same. I feel formal, perhaps authoritative. I have status. I say, "Today we're going to discuss proper etiquette." The students repeat the action and the words.

As well as once again emphasizing the influence of the outer on the inner, this exercise communicates to the students that there is no such thing as a neutral sitting position. Later on, when they're working on scenes, when they encounter a stage direction that reads, "She sits" they will know there is no standard way of sitting. They will know that how we sit often reflects what we're feeling or thinking, whom we are and what our status is at that moment. The simplest of actions, such as sitting, can convey a great deal. It should always communicate something.

After I give numerous examples, each with them copying and repeating, I change the direction of the exercise. I tell students on the count of three I will have them choose their own definitive sitting position, one that elicits a clear emotion or attitude. I then have them freeze for five seconds. When I count to five, I instruct them to whisper. I repeat this process five times: five different sitting positions and attitudes, with accompanying words. If done effectively, the students make a strong connection between what they're doing (actions) and what they're saying (words).

63. Whispered Emotions

I often have students whisper because when they do they control and own the emotion in a more dramatic way. To demonstrate this point, I do some exercises, having the students whisper many types of emotions. The students remain seated in the circle. I call out an emotion and have them sit accordingly. I have them freeze in that position; then allow them to speak, to whisper only. If I say "Anger" the students sit angrily. Of course, if there are 36 students, you see 36 different angry sitting positions, as well as facial expressions. I like to choose "angry" first because I don't want them to think angry must always be shouted. It's more unpredictable and engaging when it's whispered. I tell them, "You're still angry, you just happen to be whispering." What invariably will happen is they rely more on communicating nonverbally, and, at the same time, by holding back vocally, they stretch their inner emotional range. I typically call out 8-10 emotions, purposely choosing contrasting ones so that students are forced quickly to switch physically and emotionally.

64. Emotional Stories in Sitting Positions

The students stay seated for this one as well. I begin by once again calling out an emotion ("Amusement") and having the students strike a suitable pose. I say, "Freeze" and look around the circle for a compelling picture, and no doubt there will be many to choose from. I choose one student's pose and tell everyone else to look at him, to copy his pose. They do. I tell students that in their "amused" poses they will tell a story, allowing the position to dictate what they say. I have one student start by speaking one brief sentence. He is no longer restricted to whispering; he is free to speak in a volume of his choice. Moving clockwise, the next student—in the same position, using the same tone, same character attitude—continues the story. Now, if there are 36 students in the circle, you may not get around to everyone. Ten students (ten sentences) are usually more than sufficient.

57

While each successive student uses the same pose and character attitude, the students do not mimic each other. Their words and volume are different, as is their individual expression. What's important is that they are continuing the same emotion. After ten sentences of amusement, I stop the story. I call out another emotion ("Anxious"), and the process begins again. I continue to change as many emotions and stories that allow for everyone in the circle to have a turn at speaking.

Here's a variation: If I have 36 students, I direct the group to tell a 36- word story, on the emotion given, each student speaking one word . Or sometimes I have them speak two words at a time to create a 72-word story.

65. Using Actions to Influence Emotions

This exercise, once again, joins actions and words. It's one I incorporate into my vocals and repeats. I start with a simple sentence. "I don't want you in my life." Simple enough. I have the students add actions to this line, using hand and arm movements that reflect the following verbs: press, punch, slash, flick, pull, lift, float, bounce, wave, throw, twirl, etc. I tell the students to "press" the line, to imagine their hands are on a wall, and they are pressing against it. So the students place their hands on this imaginary wall; they press; they speak. Next I have them "punch" the line. They place their hands like a boxer's.

They jab with their left; they jab with their right; they speak. The sound is less strained than the press; it is more staccato. When they "slash" I have them imagine they're holding a sword; they slash down diagonally, left and right. The "slash" action makes the words sound like they're on a pendulum. When they "flick" I have them place their index fingers on the fleshy part of their thumbs and quickly release. The line sounds soft and airy when they do this. When they "lift" the words I have them imagine they're lifting heavy barbells. This one creates a strained sound, similar to the press. I have them "bounce" the words, as if they're bouncing a ball, and "pull" the words, as if they're engaged in a tug of war, their hands wrapped around a rope. I typically have them repeat each action and line several times before moving to the next one. Then I'll go through all of them, one at a time, quickly switching from one to the other. These actions provide the students freedom of expression and energy; they will naturally change their tones, places of emphasis, pitch, rate, and rhythm, reflecting the significance of actions on words.

66. Facial Expressions

Here's another emotion exercise, though this one has restrictions. Instead of having students strike poses, I tell them they can only use their faces. All the energy of the emotion must be expressed above the neck. First we discuss how many features make up a face. The students provide the following list: nose, eyes, eyebrows, forehead, mouth, lips, forehead, tongue, cheeks, jaw. Then I say, "I want you to express 'joy' one feature at a time." Here's how it works: I say, "Nose." They express joy in their nose. I wait three seconds, and then say, "Eyes." They express 'joy' in their eyes. I wait three seconds (and so forth). I'll go through five or six emotions, one facial feature at a time. The face is elastic, I tell them. The more they use and condition it, the more expressive it will become. Therefore this exercise is as important as any foundational one I've done.

67. Expressing Emotions Using Props

I gather for entertainment and skill development approximately 40 props in boxes and have students sit in chairs in the large circle. With help from an assistant, I pass a prop to everyone. What kind of props do I pass out? Here are some examples: an iron, broom, small lamp, bucket, teddy bear, hat, basket, blanket, clock, shovel, pot, artificial flowers, etc. I tell the students not to concern themselves too much with what prop they get. The props will be passed around, and students will wind up with many different props during the course of this exercise. I tell them the props will be used to encourage emotional expression, create character and develop story lines.

When I count to 3, I have the students pass their prop to the person sitting to their left. Now, everyone has a different prop. I continue having them pass props three or four times. Finally, I say, "Stop, this is your prop." I instruct the students to study and feel their props. I tell them I'm going to call out an emotion, and when I do I want them to begin speaking in that emotion, with exaggeration, about the prop they're holding. For instance, if I am holding the iron, and the emotion is excited, I might say something like, "Oh my god, I can't believe you bought me an iron. Now I can iron your shirts for you, morning, afternoon and night. I can be the wife you've always wanted me to be." This is a simultaneous exercise. Picture 36 students sitting in a circle, each holding a different prop, each one speaking excitedly about the prop they're holding. I have them express this emotion for about 15 seconds, long enough to speak a sentence or two. Make sure they're exaggerating. If I see or hear something particularly of interest, I might stop them after 15 seconds and have everyone watch that particular student. Good examples are always worth watching. Then they pass again and again, several times or more, until I stop them again. This time I have a broom in my possession and the emotion is disgusted. I might say something like "Sweep sweep sweep, that's all I do. When will I ever be free of these ungodly chores? When?" Then, after 15 seconds, it's time to pass again. If there are 36 students in the circle, there's a good chance students will handle approximately 9 or 10 props during the exercise. They will have explored how they can use objects to help them express emotions. Later on, when students do scenes, I require them to bring in props to enhance their emotional states. This exercise helps them make the connection between objects and feelings. It adds another dimension, gives them yet another tool they can use for discovery.

CREATING CHARACTER EXERCISES

68. Character Walks

This exercise asks students to use specific actions or characteristics, suggested by me, when they walk. I have an advanced student demonstrate first. I have him stand in a neutral position. I tell him to imagine I am holding a string attached to his head. I am pulling the string forward. His head is being pulled out. The rest of his body remains in place. This position is called the "Head First" walk. I tell him when I count to 5, I want him to assume a character and walk around the circle, his head leading the rest of his body. I also tell him to allow the rest of his body to be influenced by the position of his head. For instance, if he's walking head first, how will he move his arms? Will he swing them? Will he ball his hands near his chest? Will he take small steps, his legs close together? Will he walk flat-footed, his legs spread apart? Of course, how he walks depends largely on the character he has chosen for himself. What kind of person walks head first? What is this person thinking or feeling? Where is this person? Is he feeling a sense of urgency? Is he laid back? Asking questions is always a good way to stimulate the students' imaginations. It adds depth and weight to their choices, and, frankly, it helps them believe in what they're doing.

My assistant begins to walk, as his character. I tell the rest of the students to observe his head, his arms and legs. At some point, while he's walking, I tell my student to speak. This is one of those exercises I want him to join his body and voice because a character speaks as well as walks. As you can see, I am once again applying the outer/inner exercise I explained earlier.

After this demonstration, the rest of the students are ready to engage in this exercise. I instruct them to stand in a neutral position. I pull the imaginary string. Their heads come forward. I ask the same questions I had with my advanced student. I count to 5. They walk, as their characters, using their body parts accordingly. And then, when cued, they speak.

After they sufficiently complete the "Head First" walk, I continue with the following: "Chest First" walk; "Stomach First" walk; "Knees First" walk; "Feet First" walk. I'm sure you can create other walks. You need only observe people as your inspiration. This exercise has significant lasting effect. It not only helps them understand and appreciate the connection between the outer and the inner, but it provides them, as well, with tools they can use later when they are engaged in scene work, or even when they're creating characters in musicals or plays.

69. Physical Switches

The format for this one is much the same as the Emotional Switches I mentioned in an earlier exercise. This time I move around the circle, handing each student a card that names a physical description, such as the following:

- You have a bent back
- You walk with a limp
- You must walk straight because your neck is stiff
- You arms are very itchy
- You have pain in your legs, you walk with very small steps
- You hunch forward and rub your hands together as you walk
- You waddle from side to side as you walk
- You skip as you walk

Once everyone knows his physical description, I have an advanced student or assistant collect the cards. I have my students walk around with their physical characteristic, perhaps 15 seconds or so. This exercise, by the way, is a "movement only" exercise; make sure students are not talking, unless directed to do so. I instruct them to greet each other, however they see fit, given their condition. After they greet each other with a handshake, they switch characteristics. The students then walk around in their new positions for 15 seconds, until they once again meet and greet someone else, and the process continues. I have them switch at least ten times.

70. Mimicking Physical Characteristics

I give out and then collect cards, as I did in the previous exercise. This one involves mimic and repeats. Therefore, I tell everyone to watch each other and listen carefully. One at a time, I have students walk—with their condition—to the center of the circle. The student is instructed to stop, speak a brief sentence, and then walk back to his position in the circle. Everyone in the circle will then repeat the same walk, the same words. I guide the students, asking questions, before I have them begin. For instance, if I am the student who received the "you walk with a limp" card, I might ask these questions: How does it feel walking with a limp? Have I had it a long time? Or is it recent? How did I get it? It's important that they internalize what they are doing externally. It's also important, as we know by now, to allow the external to influence the internal.

If I have 36 students in the circle, as I normally do, I will not have time for everyone to perform this exercise, especially since mimics and repeats follow each one. Typically, I'll call on 10-12 students. That's more than sufficient to satisfy the intent of the exercise: to have each student, through mimic and repeats, experience 10-12 physical descriptions, character walks, with accompanying verbal expressions.

71. Character Building

As a variation to the previous exercises—or extensions of them—I give the students character cards. For instance, they receive cards with character types, such as the following: Italian chef, basketball coach, body builder, librarian, rock star, hot dog vendor, etc. Once they know their character type, I collect the cards. I tell students they must come up with a defining physical feature for the character they receive. I'll take them through exercises such as this one: "On the count of three, find a face for this character, concentrate on the lips, the mouth, the eyebrows, etc. What are his arms and hands doing? Does he stand tall and straight or hunched over? How does he walk? Fast? Slow? Confident? Shy?"

What I'm asking them to do—which is a departure from exercise 1—is make a choice. After they choose a defining characteristic, I instruct them to walk around and eventually switch characters with one another, using the same format as the Physical Switches. I may also integrate the Character Mimic into this one: have them walk and speak as their character types, and then have everyone else mimic and repeat. This exercise, as well as the previous two, prepares students for specific character improvisations and scenes they will perform, as outlined in Sections 2-4.

72. Nonverbal Status Work using Playing Cards

I have the students sit in chairs in a large circle. Each student receives a playing card. It's important that no one else sees the card. I tell the students to sit according to the number they get. The higher the number, the greater the status. The lowest card is a 2. If I am a 2, what kind of person would I be, to have such low status? How would I sit to reveal that status? The same can be said for the high status cards: Jack, Queen, King, Ace. What kind of person would I be if I were one of these cards? How would I sit? After I give out the cards, I direct them to make a choice. I count to ten. They strike a sitting position and freeze.

I exclude one student from receiving a card. He is the guesser. When everyone is in a freeze, he goes around the circle, guessing what playing card each student received, based on his sitting position. I ask anyone who was guessed correctly to stand up. Sometimes, I use a variation. I have two guessers. It's interesting when their guesses are off by quite a bit, such as one seeing a 10, the other seeing a 5. I have them explain. Whichever variation I use, I collect the cards and start the process over again, repeating it four or five times, with new guessers each time.

73. Character Mimics

I use a two-line format, dividing the class into 18 students on each side, facing each other, about fifteen feet apart. The emphasis is on character development and mimic. I approach one of the lines, giving each student a characteristic: head forward, chest forward, knees leading, stomach out, itchy arms, bent back, limp, etc. The first exercise is a simple mimic. The first student in line walks 7-8 feet, his head forward. He stops. The student across from him assumes the same characteristic, the same walk. He freezes, facing the student across from him, a foot away. This exercise continues with students 2-18, down the line, moving with their unique characteristics, each one mimicked by someone across from them.

74. Character Mimics with Speaking

This one is similar, except here the lead student speaks after he walks and stops. I remind students of the outer/inner work they've already done. I use the first characteristic in line as an example. If someone is walking head first, it has to influence what he says and how he says it: the texture and sound quality of his voice. I instruct the students to begin. The "head first" student walks 7-8 feet, stops, and says, with appropriate gesture, "Look at all those birds in the tree." The student across from him, mimics his actions —as he did in the previous exercise—and his words. I have students continue zig zagging, until the last student in line mimics the last lead student.

75. Question/Answer, Same Characteristics

The format remains the same, with students in two lines, standing across from each other. This one is a partial mimic, but students do not repeat what each other says. Here's an example: The "head first" student walks and stops. This time, though, he asks a question directly to the student opposite him. "Excuse me, have you seen my glasses?" The student across from him assumes the same characteristic (head first). He walks up to the lead student, using the same actions, stops and—this time—answers. "Yes, they're on your face." Here, you have two "head first" people meeting. However, they are different people, not the same. As with the previous exercises, I continue this exercise until all the students have participated.

76. Question/Answer, Different Characteristics

Here's a variation of the previous exercise: I sometimes give students opposite each other different characteristics. For instance, if the first student is head first, I make the student across from him chest first. In this scenario, if the first student asks, "Excuse me, have you seen my glasses?" the chest first student—influenced by his unique characteristic—might say, in response, "Yes, I believe I just stepped on them, for they were in my way." While this one and the previous exercise are equally beneficial for skill development, this latter one may have more entertainment value.

77. Character Development

For this one, I return to character cards I used in earlier exercises. I give each student a card and tell him on the count of three to begin walking around, finding the physical life of his character. Before I count to three—and this is something I always do when giving out characters—I have them close their eyes while I ask questions: where are you right now? What kind of day has it been? What just happened to you? Were your expectations for the day met? Do you have any fears or disappointments? What is your greatest hope? I don't give them a physical mannerism or quality, just a character type, so they have to answer these questions in their head, use their imaginations and refer to the many exercises we've done to this point. I instruct them to open their eyes and walk. After a quick foray around the stage, I bring them back to the circle and give them a sentence to repeat. "My gosh, I didn't expect today to turn out the way it did." I purposely give a sentence that is general and vague, something anyone, regardless of specific character type, might say. Now I have the students walk again, as their characters, this time whispering the line I gave them. Everyone is whispering the same line, yet it looks like 36 different people walking around. Once again, I bring the students back to the large circle. I tell them that, one at a time, they will walk to the center of the circle, as their character, and say the line.

I have the student immediately to my right begin. Perhaps his character card reads Superhero. He walks ten feet, to the middle of the circle, stops and says, "My, gosh, I didn't expect today to turn out the way it did." He then returns to the large circle. The exercise continues clockwise. The next student's character card reads Fairy. She walks ten feet, to the middle of the circle, stops and says, "My, gosh, I didn't expect today to turn out the way it did." She then returns to the large circle. I offer the first two examples to show how varied and exciting this exercise can be. Obviously a superhero and a fairy would walk and talk differently, would have different motivations and points of reference for saying the line.

While this last exercise departs in format from the first four, they share the same objective: character development. I just happen to use varied ways of encouraging and meeting this objective. In the end, what matters is that students are experimenting with movement, words and emotions. Most importantly, they are making discoveries under the guise of imaginative play. Of course, it's a much different play than what you might see and hear in a playground. The play here is controlled (and directed), and in this environment they learn, without consciously knowing that that's what they're doing.

78. Using Costume Accessories

This exercise focuses on the use of costume pieces to engage students' imaginations and further influence outer/inner choices. As well as having boxes and shelves of props, I keep racks of clothing and boxes of assorted accessories. Here's what I mean by costume accessories: hats, gloves, scarves, shirts, jackets, glasses, cape, coats, etc. It wouldn't be hard to assemble these in a short period of time; one or two trips to a thrift store should suffice. These exercises are similar to the prop exercises, with the exception that the students wear, rather than hold, something.

I start by having students stand in a large circle. They're going to need to move, because most of what I do with costumes relates to creating character, and this must be done through movement and actions. In the center of the circle I have two or three large boxes, containing items such as I mentioned earlier. I explain to the students that I will begin passing around the costume pieces. When I say, "Stop" the costume piece they have in their possession, will be the first one with which they experiment.

I pass out the costumes and have them pass them around several times before I say, "Stop." I instruct the students to "wear what you have." They do. Then—as is my custom—I ask questions: who are you? Where are you? What is happening at this moment? What is your state of mind, your attitude? At the count of five, they strike a pose, having made a choice about character. Then I count to five and tell to move about the stage, revealing their characters. After they move around for thirty seconds, I stop them and tell them when I count to five they can resume walking. This time I direct them to speak, in a whisper so that they class doesn't become too loud. I don't have them speak very long, just enough to develop an emotional life, as influenced by the costume accessory. The students find comfort in this exercise, since they most likely experienced playing dress up as children, pretending to be someone other than themselves. This exercise taps into that natural source of energy and creativity that many of them, perhaps, forgot about. After I stop the students, I have them return to the circle, at which time I have them pass their costumes around the circle several times, until I stop them and start the process all over again. I usually do this exercise enough times so that students wind up wearing five or six costume accessories, and creating as many characters.

79. Costume Switches

The process for this one begins the same as the previous one. Students pass around the costume accessories until I tell them to stop and proceed to wear the one they're holding. Then I take them through the same process: ask them questions, have them strike a pose, then have them walk. And this is where the change takes place for this exercise. I have them walk for thirty seconds. Then I tell them to make a connection with someone else. This connection can be a simple handshake or a word or two. After the connection is made, the students exchange their costume accessories, and in doing so, their characters. I have them repeat this process 8-10 times, meaning they wear and experience many costume accessories and walk around, suggesting character as many times.

80. Simultaneous Character Speaking

Here's another simple variation: everyone in the circle receives a costume accessory. I count to three; they pose. Then on the next count to three, I tell them to speak a line or two, simultaneously. They don't need to move around to do this one. They stay in the circle and speak, gesticulating as necessary to convey character.

81. One-at-a-Time Character Speaking

Sometimes I choose to have them speak one at a time, rather than simultaneously. I do this either of two ways. In the first scenario, I simply have them go around the circle, each student expressing his character through costume and words. In the second scenario, I have them do a story-telling exercise. The first student starts the story, speaking a line from his point of view. The next student, a different character, continues the story, changing it only to suit his personality. The rest of the students continue appropriately. At some point—if the story gets too crazy—I may start a different story, continuing in the circle where the previous student ended.

82. Mimicking Character Actions

The focus is once again on creating character, this time through the use of mimic exercises. I have students observe each other and then mimic each other's actions, including voice inflection, repetitive mannerisms, repeated phrases, etc. They begin by sitting in a large circle. If 36 students are doing little more than sitting, I guarantee you will see 36 different sitting positions. Some will cross their legs, some will slouch, some will sit straight, some will have their head in their hands. You will see a great deal of idiosyncratic positions. So I say to the class, "You see the way Raoul is sitting. Everyone sit like him." They do. Or I say, "You see the way Rayleen has her arm? Place your arm just like hers." They do. Then I have everyone sit and talk to themselves, talk the way they normally would in conversation. I notice many mannerisms, ticks, especially in the head, the arms, the hands. I stop them, and have everyone look at one student as he talks to himself. I tell the class, "Listen to his voice, watch his arms and hands, the tilt of his head. Listen to and watch everything."

The students then mimic the student I point out. This exercise is a natural predecessor to the next one, where students will work more closely with one another.

83. Switching Roles

I divide the class into pairs and give them a task. I instruct them to find a space in the theater for five to seven minutes, wherein I want them to take turns talking to each other about something they did, something they'd like to do, something of a personal nature, within reason. What they say is less important than how they say it. I tell each speaker to be conscious of highlighting their vocal, verbal and nonverbal characteristics while they're speaking. In other words, I want them to give the other person something to watch and hear. I tell them they can't merely sit and talk. They must stand up, they must gesticulate, try to talk excitedly. If it's a story they're telling, it should include actions and expression. I demonstrate. When I talk I tilt and move my head, I use my arms, my voice inflects in wild ways, I have a certain texture in my voice, a quality. First I tell them to listen, get the quality of the voice, get the rhythm, get the cadence. Then they should watch closely for mannerisms they can mimic and use. They need only talk for 3-5 minutes each. The observation is the critical part. The student who's listening and watching is taking mental notes. He must memorize the other student.

Here's the reason why: when they finish talking to each other, revealing details about themselves, they will introduce themselves as the other person. Let's assume John and Mike are a pair. John talks expressively for 3-5 minutes, gesticulating, moving, as he does so. Mike listens intently to John's unique voice patterns; he watches closely his idiosyncratic movements and mannerisms. It's Mike's turn next to speak. John observes.

When it's time for the student's to present, Mike and John go on stage, and Mike introduces John, speaking and moving as John. I suppose you can say he becomes John. And then John introduces Mike, becoming Mike in voice and actions as he does.

To make this one as much of a stretch as possible for the students, I choose the pairs based on physical features, voice quality, personality, etc. I mix the largest boy with the smallest girl. I mix the student with the thickest ethnic accent with the student who has the clearest pronunciation. I mix the so-called "trouble maker" with the model student. In other words, I take students out of their comfort zone for this exercise. I want them to get out of themselves, live in someone else's skin for a while, and the results are always startlingly entertaining and beneficial. I am always amazed at their skill, when put to the task. This exercise will take a while, most of the period, if you have 18 pairs. Sometimes, out of necessity, I have to limit how long they can speak, both before and during the presentation.

Dramatic work is not magic. It's work. This is the message I tell my students. Much of what actors do—in terms of creating character—has its basis in the observation of human behavior. They watch; they listen; they're aware of their surroundings and the people in them. This exercise aims to train my students to be attentive to what they see and hear —and then use what they see and hear. I'm not looking for perfection in this exercise. If my students capture even something small—the slightest texture of the voice, the slightest tilt of the head or arm, the fidgety feet, the demure stance—it means they are opening up a treasure trove of discoveries. They are storing detail and memory, all of which can be used at a later time as they use their imaginations, create characters, and, in the process, learn more about themselves and the world around them.

84. Creating Group Pictures Using Costumes

After everyone has a costume accessory, I tell the students the objective in this exercise is to create a group picture that creates a sensible story. One student, wearing a trench coat, starts by walking to the center of the circle. He stops and poses. Someone in the circle, wearing a scarf, has an idea. She enters the picture, loops her arm under the student's arm. Another student, wearing a fur, enters, looks at the man and woman, points at them. The picture is becoming clear. There is some kind of love triangle here. You can see the possibilities in this exercise.

If the picture seems complete, I might stop it. Otherwise, I'll have other students enter, as well. Of course, who enters and why they enter has something to do with what they're wearing. The costume accessories have to match in some way for the picture to work. I usually leave this one up to the ingenuity of the students. Once the picture gets started, the students will come up with ideas. After each picture, I have students pass around their costumes again. Typically, I have the class create as many as five pictures.

85. Adding Voices to Group Pictures

Sometimes, often unplanned, I'll add voices to the pictures. For instance, take the picture I just described: the love triangle. Since the picture appears to hold intrigue and mystery, I'm suddenly interested to know more about it. Before anyone else enters from the circle, I say, "Stop, I want the three of you to speak." The students engage in a short scene, influenced by their costumes and the picture they created.

Possibilities abound when students wear costume accessories. The reason is simple: the students' imaginations are engaged and stimulated, and when this occurs the possibility for magic becomes ever more present and viable. My job is to be attentive to the students' creativity, their genius—to know when to tap into it, and then watch, listen, appreciate and enjoy. It is, for me, beauty manifest.

Having students wear costume accessories will encourage the outer/inner connection as much as any exercise. Still, there's an equally important reason for these exercises. Seeing the effect costumes have on performers and audience, the students will, later on, seek out costumes for their own scenes because the bottom line is this: costume accessories help the performers believe in their characters, as well as where they are, and what they're doing. And if the performers believe, the audience will, as well.

CONCENTRIC CIRCLE EXERCISE

86. Concentric Circle

This one uses a circle-within-circle format, designed to have all students performing at the same time, while interacting with many different partners. As well as being a desirable large group activity, it's an opportunistic way to review most of the earlier exercises related to voice, character, movement, genres, gibberish, storytelling, mimic, mirror, etc. It's a high- energy activity, and ideal if you want complete group participation without singling anyone out. The group, in pairs, is participating, to the best of their abilities, and they're drawing energy from a variety of students in the class. Here's how it works: If I have 36 students, I place 18 students in the outer circle and 18 students in the inner circle. To start the exercise, one outer student faces one inner student. In other words, everyone has a partner. I tell the students that the inner circle is going to remain where it is. The outer circle will move one space to the left (or clockwise) when I tell them to move.

This one, I have to warn you, can get noisy because 17 pairs will be interacting simultaneously. It's important that students keep their interactions with each other reasonable, not too loud, because throughout the activity I stop what they're doing and change the direction. I'm going to provide a sample lesson in its entirety. Keep in mind that what I write here is just an example, since each time I do this exercise I change the directions.

Direction #1: "Perform a 1 minute mirror exercise. The outer person is the leader. Use neutral expression, eyes on eyes and slow hand movements." After one minute, stop.
Direction #2: "Outer group, move one space to your left. You now have a new partner. Inner person communicates in gibberish, outer person translates. You must whisper. When I say switch, you switch roles. Okay, you have 2 minutes. Ready, begin." After 2 minutes, I say, "Stop."

<u>Direction #3</u>: "Outer group, move one space to your left. You now have a new partner. Situational improvisation. The inner person is excited, you shake hands with the outer person, but the outer person is upset with you. You have 2 minutes. Ready, begin." After 2 minutes, I say, "Stop."

<u>Direction #4</u>: "Outer group, move one space to your left. You now have a new partner. Voice exercise. Reunion, after a long separation. Inner person talks in a high pitch, outer in a low pitch. I say switch; you switch roles. You have 2 minutes. Ready, begin." After 2 minutes, I say, "Stop."

<u>Direction #5</u>: "Outer group, move one space to the your left. You now have a new partner. Laughing and crying exercise. Inner person starts out laughing, outer person crying. When I say switch, you switch roles. You have 2 minutes. Ready, begin." After 2 minutes, I say, "Stop."

<u>Direction #6</u>: "Outer group, move one space to your left. You now have a new partner. Use your imaginations. Inner person, you bought a new toy, it comes with a remote. Outer person you are the toy. You move to the instructions inner person gives you. You have 2 minutes. Ready, begin." After 2 minutes, I say, "Stop."

<u>Direction #7</u>: "Outer group, move one space to your left. You now have a new partner. Stand back to back, telephone conversation, emotion switches. Speak in whispers. I will call out emotions, switch accordingly. You have 2 minutes. Ready, begin." (I start with mysterious, then switch to funny, then switch to angry, then switch to confused.) After 2 minutes, I say, "Stop."

<u>Direction #8</u>: "Outer group, move one space to your left. You now have a new partner. Mirror exercise with actions in slow motion. Inner person does the following actions: comb your hair, put on makeup, brush your teeth, all in slow motion. Outer person follows. You have 2 minutes. Ready, begin." After 2 minutes, I say, "Stop."

<u>Direction #9</u>: "Outer group, move one space to the left. You

now have a new partner. Pattern story. Have a conversation according to this pattern: 1, 2, 3, 4, 1, 2, 3, 4, etc. Inner person says one word, outer person says one word, then continue with 2, 3, 4, and back again. You have 2 minutes. Ready, begin." After 2 minutes I say, "Stop."

Direction #10: "Outer group, move one space to the left. You now have a new partner. Physical positions, outer/inner. Inner person stand with folded arms, with a frown on your face. Outer person rub your hands, excitedly. Use these positions to influence what you say in a 2 minute improvisation. Ready, begin." After 2 minutes, I say, "Stop."

Direction #11: "Outer group moves one space to the left. You now have a new partner. Physical positions, outer/inner. Outer person stands with hands on his hips, inner person covers his ears, looks away. Use these positions to influence what you say in a 2 minute improvisation. Ready, begin." After 2 minutes, I say, "Stop."

Direction #12: "Outer group moves one space to the left. You now have a new partner. Alphabet story. Inner starts the conversation by beginning a sentence with "A". Outer follows with a "B" sentence. Keep going until you finish the alphabet. Ready, begin. After 2 minutes, I say, "Stop."

For Directions 13-17, I instruct the outer group to get chairs and sit down. The inner group remains standing.

Direction #13: "Outer group moves one space to the left. You now have a new partner. Outer person sits in chair. Here's the situation: A public place, such as a park, inner person returns from the bathroom to find that someone is sitting in his chair. He wants his chair back. Outer person doesn't want to give it back. Ready, begin." After 2 minutes, I say, "Stop."

Direction #14: "Outer group moves one space to the left. You now have a new partner. This time the inner person sits, the outer stands. Physical positions, outer/inner. In-

76

ner person sits bent over, head down, hands on his face. Outer person stands, with hand on inner person's shoulder. Use these positions to influence what you say in a 2 minute improvisation. Ready, begin." After 2 minutes, I say, "Stop."

Direction #15: "Outer group moves one space to the left. You now have a new partner. Outer person sits. You are a child who doesn't want to play with anyone. Inner person, you are the teacher, trying to get the child to get up and play with others. Ready, begin." After 2 minutes, I say, "Stop."

Direction #16: "Outer group moves one space to the left. You now have a new partner. Inner person sits. You are a new patient at a dentist's office. Outer person, you are the dentist. You speak in a foreign accent and have an unorthodox way of performing dentistry. Ready, begin." After 2 minutes, I say, "Stop."

Direction #17: "Outer group moves one space to the left. You now have a new partner. Outer person sits. You are an old person who's having trouble standing or walking. Inner person, you are the caretaker or physical therapist, trying to get the person to get up and move. Ready, begin." After 2 minutes, I say, "Stop."

This one, as I said, is high energy and a workout, for everyone involved.. If the conditions and requirements are not set, this one can become chaotic. To succeed with this one, I have to be clear and authoritative with my directions, and the students have to willingly receive them. It's not something I can do in the first week. I can only do it when I know my students have been fully conditioned. While it's an exhausting exercise, it is one of the more rewarding ones because the students' energy and imaginations are at a peak. Furthermore, during the course of the workout, they are reviewing and developing many of the skills that were covered in the previous exercises.

EXERCISES USING MUSIC

87. Nonverbal Expression using Music

This exercise uses recorded music, ideally classical music or movie soundtracks, or anything void of words. Years ago —before the explosion of digital technology—I brought in compact discs and a playback machine. To change music meant I, or someone else, had to physically remove a disc and replace it with another. The changing times have made this exercise easier to execute. Now I rely on a student to compile music tracks and edit, as well, on his laptop. In fact, I place the full responsibility of changing the music throughout in the hands of this student. I instruct this student to find music that has dramatic shifts in tone. I ask him to compile and edit 30-45 second extractions, thereby making the shift from track to track smooth and efficient.

Here's how it goes: I place students in a large circle and tell them I'm going to play music and change it quite frequently. Their job, as always, is to follow my directions. I tell them to close their eyes. I play a Beethoven piece. I tell them to listen, just absorb it. I ask questions: what is the mood? The atmosphere? The tone? If you were in the world of this music who or what would you be? Where would you be? Make a choice, I tell them. When I count to five, I want them to open their eyes, to use only their face and eyes to show the story of the music.

I allow them ten seconds of facial expression. Then I tell them when I count to five they can add their right arm/hand. After ten more seconds I tell them they can add their left arm/hand. Then after ten more seconds they can use their back and their legs. Finally after ten more seconds I tell them they can move, slowly. I tell them to let the music dictate how they move, where they move, why they move. The movement should never be random, with no connection to setting and character. I want them to tell a story: to be someone, in a specific place and time. They must, of course, coordinate all their actions and movements with the music. It's important to note that the students are working independently here. They are not interacting. This exercise may seem, written out, to be a long process, but, in actuality, it's probably no more than a minute or two, beginning to end. After I stop the music I bring the students back to the circle and have them shake out their hands and legs. I then repeat the process with another piece of music that is different in tone and dramatic appeal than the first one. I continue with this exercise, changing the music five or six times.

88. Creating Nonverbal Stories with Music

This one adds one variation to the previous exercise. I guide students through the same process, and then right before I instruct them to move, I change the direction of the exercise. It becomes interactive, though only nonverbally so. I tell them to move on stage, in their story, for ten seconds and then naturally find one or two others who seem to be in a world similar to theirs. They shouldn't force this connection, however. It should happen organically. And, of course, it's a silent activity; therefore, they cannot talk with others. They must rely on a sense, a vibe, that their world, their story, should join with another's. To make this happen, one of the students must relent to the other. There cannot be two stories at one time. One story remains; the only difference now is that there are two (or perhaps even three) people in the story. When they do find one or two partners I tell them to find a space where they can explore their story, without distraction. This one is more of a challenge for the students, but it also carries greater reward because the students are working organically together, without words, and when it works it appears as if ordained by the gods of drama. This is especially true when I see 10-12 stories developing simultaneously on stage: students moving silently, together, while communicating a story influenced by music.

Music provides wonderful opportunities to further enhance verbal and nonverbal communication. Besides it helps students develop an ear, draw a relationship between what they're hearing and what they're doing. It's a language everyone understands. In Section 2, I will describe a two-person improvisation that picks up where these exercises leave off. I recommend you compile and edit music for use in your classroom. It will result in exciting lessons that will teach and entertain.

89. Introduction to Jazz Shakespeare

Allow me to explain the origin of this exercise. Years ago, I was teaching an English class (I taught AP English for 15 years), and we were reading Macbeth. I had many of the school's jazz musicians in my class, so one day we went to the theater. I had them bring their instruments (trumpet, saxophone, drum, clarinet, violin, guitar, etc.). They played, and the class read. They kept changing the key, the tone, the mood, the speed, the rhythm, the beat and atmosphere. They played mostly jazz, sometimes blues. The readers followed wherever the musicians traveled. The class found itself celebrating jazz and Shakespeare at the same time. A discovery was made, giving birth to a title.

Since then, music and language, in combination, have been a staple in my drama class. Here's how Jazz Shakespeare works: I give students Shakespearean lines and tell them they're going to speak and coordinate language with the music they hear. In other words, read to the beat, the rhythm, the mood and tone. Go where the music goes. If you use live music, you have to plan ahead. First, you will need to find students who can play, and then you will need to schedule them into your class. Of course, if you're lucky, you may have some players in your class. If you don't have musicians, you can do this exercise with recorded music. The results will be similarly effective, but, to be honest, it is more interesting and exciting for everyone involved—readers, class and musicians—if you can do it live. If, however, you have no choice but to use recorded music, you will have to do something similar to what you did when you used music for nonverbal movement and storytelling. You will have to find and edit music. While jazz or blues are preferable, it doesn't even have to be music, traditionally speaking. It can be sounds, something ambient, as long as it sets a mood or a tone and keeps changing, and as long as it gives the students something to follow and use. In any case, you're going to need Shakespearean language. Since I made reference to Macbeth, here are examples of lines from that play that I give to students on small strips of paper:

"Is this a dagger which I see before me, the handle toward my hand? Come, let me clutch thee! I have thee not, and yet I see thee still. Art thou not, fatal vision, sensible to feeling as to sight? Or art thou but a dagger of the mind, a false creation proceeding from the heat-oppressed brain?"

"Will all Neptune's ocean wash this blood clean from my hand? No. This my hand will rather the multitudinous seas incarnadine, making the green one red."
"What are these, so withered, and so wild in their attire, that look not like the inhabitants of the earth, and yet are on it? You should be women, and yet your beards forbid me to interpret that you are so."

"By clock 'tis day, and yet dark night strangles the travel-ing lamp. Is it night's predominance, or the day's shame, that darkness does the face of earth entomb when living light should kiss it?"

"Awake, awake! Ring the alarum bell. Murder and trea-son! Banquo and Donalbain! Malcolm! Awake! Shake off this downy sleep, death's counterfeit,, and look on death itself!"

"Come, seeling night, scarf up the tender eye of pitiful day, and with thy bloody and invisible hand cancel and tear to pieces that great bond which keeps me pale. Light thickens, and the crow makes wing to the rooky wood."

"His virtues will plead like angels, trumpet-tongued against the deep damnation of his taking off; and pity, like a naked new-born babe, striding the blast, or heaven's cherubin, horsed upon the sightless couriers of

the air, shall blow the horrid deed in every eye, that tears shall drown the wind."

When everyone has a line, I have the class practice collectively, walking around the stage, sharing only their lines with each other. Soon after, I assemble the group in a circle. It's not mandatory that they memorize their lines; they can use the strip of paper. If I want them to memorize the line, I would have to give the lines a day earlier.

I instruct the musicians to play. Simultaneously, I have the students speak their lines with the music. A minute later, the musicians change the tone, rhythm and mood. The students speak their line again. I continue this process at least a dozen times, noticing how the lines change—as the music does—each time. Sometimes pauses are added; sometimes special emphasis is given; sometimes it's faster or slower. Always, it's rhythmically and tonally different.

90. Jazz Shakespeare for Individual Speakers

This time the students speak their lines individually, standing in front of a live microphone., which I place center stage, in the middle of the circle. I have the students, one at a time, move to the microphone, say their line, coordinated with whatever music the band is playing, and then return to the circle. If I want to add some style to this exercise, I create a much different format. I have the students bring out tables, simulating a club atmosphere, minus the cigar smoke. In this scenario, the microphone stand is placed downstage center. I turn on stage lights, making the theater dim, providing atmosphere to go along with the musical atmosphere and the sound of Shakespearean language. I have students from various tables get up, one at a time, and speak at the microphone. The musicians change what they're playing for each new student. If I want to add a further touch to this one, I can bring out the costume boxes and give hats, scarves, jackets, etc. to the students. This exercise, I realize, takes effort and a willingness to stretch the boundaries of what a classroom looks and sounds like, but, trust me, it's an exercise the students will long remember. Besides, they're experiencing Shakespeare without the normal analytical weight. Here the language is associated with music, lights, costumes and celebration.

91. Jazz Shakespeare in Pairs

I copy for everyone the same scene: Act 2, Macbeth and Lady Macbeth. He comes down the steps after having just killed the king. He is distraught; she is nervous. It is dark; an owl shrieks. It's a wonderful scene to read while having the musicians play. I have the pairs spread out. For this reading, because of the scene's foreboding nature, I have the musicians play something dark, perhaps just ambient sounds. I definitely don't want something melodic sounding here. Maybe it begins with a sustained note from a saxophone, and then a string from a violin, maybe a drum, banged quietly, as if coming from far away. I have the musicians experiment with mood. The students can speak their lines to this changing mood in any number of ways. I can keep them in a large circle and have them read simultaneously. I can have them move up to the microphone, one pair at a time, and read a part of the scene, and then have another pair continue where the previous pair left off. Or I can go right back to the club setting. I can place four students at a table. The lines from the scene can move around the tables, each pair speaking ten or twelve lines, until the scene ends.

What's important, regardless of format—or whether you use student musicians or recordings—is the joining of music and Shakespearean language. Speaking the language itself, regardless of supplementing it with sound, is already musical since Shakespeare wrote poetry with the ear of a musician. The point is this: I want my students to associate the speaking of language, not just Shakespeare, with something musical and beautiful. Later on, when they perform scenes and monologues, I want them to do so with the remembrance of music in their ears. I want them to know that they can supply their own music, with their own voices and their motivation to create beauty in sound.

STAGING EXERCISES

92. Learning Stage Areas

In concluding Section 1, I now depart from performance-based exercises that directly encourage the development of vocal, verbal and nonverbal communication. The following exercises are more technical and mechanical, though easily as critical as anything I've addressed up to this point because they're related to staging. With that said, let me make this clear: staging would be impossible to explain or describe in a day or a month. It's an ongoing process that requires patience, practice and a trained eye, developed primarily from experience. An understanding of staging is an intensive study unto itself. Therefore, out of respect to its complexity, I will not address it here. What I can write about, however, are the prerequisites to staging. Students need to learn about stage positions, about the areas of a theatrical stage, and about what it means to "give stage" and to "take stage."

I have students sit downstage and watch as I have my assistants demonstrate where the following stage areas are located:

- Downstage Left
- Middle Left
- Upstage Left
- Upstage Center
- Middle Center
- Downstage Center
- Downstage Right
- Middle Right
- Upstage Right

I make sure everyone understands that "Down" means towards them (the audience) and "Up" means further away, towards the cyclorama wall. They also need to know that when they hear "Left" or "Right" it is the actor's left or right, not the audience's. Observing my assistants walk from area to area, the students can see that a stage has significant depth and width. I tell them, later on, they are going to need to use depth and width when staging scenes.

I choose students, one at a time, and give them directions. "Stand Upstage Center...Stand Downstage Right...Stand Upstage Right...Stand Downstage Left... Stand Downstage Center..." After having a handful of students stand in the nine stage areas, I choose other students to name the areas. I say, "I'm going to move around the stage; when I stop, you name the area." I stand Downstage Left. A student says "Downstage Left." I stand Upstage Center, another student says, "Upstage Center." I continue until I stand in every area. Each time I do, a different student identifies the area. Whichever approach I use, it's important I take my time and don't rush through this learning phase. What they do later on, during the "Beyond" stage of the class, is dependent on their understanding these areas.

93. Learning Standing Positions

While the class watches, I have one of my assistants demonstrate. I have her start in a neutral position, facing the class, head straight, eyes centered, arms at side. I tell the class this one is a Full Front position. I have her move her right leg 45 degrees to the right. Her left leg remains in place. I tell the students this one is a One Quarter Right position. Next I have her move her left leg parallel with the right. She now stands in a Profile Right position. I instruct her to move her fight leg another 45 degrees, while the left remains in place. She now stands in a Three Quarter Right position. Finally, as I have her swing her left leg to meet her right, she stands in a Full Back position, her back to the audience. I then have my assistant start again in a Full Front position, repeating the same movements, this time to the left: One Quarter Left, Profile Left, Three Quarter Left, Full Back. Now I have the entire class stand up, back in a large circle, to practice these stage positions. I give directions: "Full Front position." I check to make sure everyone has this one. "One Quarter Left," I say. They move accordingly. I check again. I continue calling out stage positions, checking for their accuracy. After I go through all the positions, certain of their understanding, I have them sit downstage again.

Now I combine their understanding of stage positions and stage areas. I choose students one at a time to go on stage. I give directions to the first student: "Stand Downstage Right in a One Quarter Left position." He fulfills the direction perfectly. I choose another student. "Stand Upstage Left in a Three Quarter Right position." He figures it out correctly. To speed up the process, I often choose two students at a time. "Stand Downstage Center in a Full Back position." In this case, both students stand, side by side, their backs to the audience. This exercise takes a while because I want everyone in the class to stand on stage in specified standing positions. The more they practice, the more these terms and positions become part of their drama vocabulary.

94. Learning to Give, Take, and Share

I place two chairs Middle Center and have the class sit downstage. I ask my assistants, or two advanced students, to sit on the chairs. I say three very important words: "Give, Take, Share." I have the two students demonstrate. I have sit, turned 45 degrees toward each other, both chairs on the same plane. "This is a Shared position," I tell the class. "Neither student has more emphasis than the other. There are times, however, we want one of them to have more emphasis than the other. They can do this either of two ways. One of them can give stage to the other, or one of them can take stage." I tell one student to stand up, to move upstage left of the seated student, to stand in a Full Front position. I tell the seated student to turn her body (and, thus, her head) upstage left to look at the student standing upstage of her. I tell the class the student standing has "taken stage," meaning she has taken a stronger position of focus and emphasis. I tell the class why (and when) it's necessary to take stage. For instance, if this student has something important to say, if she's speaking a monologue, she wants to stand out. The more she's seen, the more she'll be heard. Now I have her sit again, and both students are back in a Shared position. This time I have her stand up and move Downstage Left. I tell her to stand in a Three Quarter Right position. She does. She has just "given stage" to the seated student, who is now in a Full Front position (and, thus, has more emphasis). In this situation the girl standing anticipates that the girl seated has something important, such as a monologue, to say. Therefore, she moves down and looks up, and in doing so allows the other student the "stage." If she is Downstage Right, looking up at the seated girl, it would be a terrible position for her to talk because her back would be the audience. The general rule, I tell my students, is "do not turn your back to the audience. If you find yourself on stage with your back to the audience and you need to speak lines, make an adjustment. Move upstage of the other person. Take stage, so you'll be seen and heard."

95. Practicing Give, Take, and Share in Pairs

I divide students into pairs, have them go on stage one pair at a time to practice give, take and shared. Here's an example of the directions I give: "John and Paul, show a shared position." They stand in One Quarter positions, facing each other. Then I say, "Okay, both of you are sitting down. Paul, I want you to take stage." They sit down. Then Paul stands up, moves upstage of the chairs, and stands directly over John. "Well done," I say. "Now, stay where you are. John, I want you to take stage." John gets up and moves upstage right, stands in a Full Front position. "Well done," I say. "Paul, give stage to John." Paul, who has been in a Full Front position, standing over the chairs, now turns his body in a Three Quarter Right position, facing John. "Well done," I say.

I go through this same procedure with as many pairs as I can in a single day, and if I run out of time I'll continue the next day. This work is too important to short change it. Students need this rudimentary understanding of staging scenes. They need to know that a scene is never static, that the balance of power, of focus and emphasis, is in constant flux. It's give and take, and the actors' movements—their sitting and standing positions—must reflect this fluid change.

These exercises introduce to my students a necessary component of my drama class. Without a basic knowledge of stage areas, standing positions, and the "give and take" of staging, all the previous work would be limited in its effectiveness. As I alluded to earlier, staging requires practice and continued observation and exposure to how others do it. It must be studied before it can be perfected, if such an ideal is even possible. As the year proceeds, as the students perform more and more, they will develop an eye for what works and what doesn't. Words such as "depth, plane, width, height, balance and composition" will become part of their everyday drama vocabulary. This learning will not take place suddenly. It will develop gradually, as all learning must. But what's important is the foundation for this learning has been established. The students can now build upon what they know. Soon, as they enter the "beyond" stage, in Sections 2-4, they will direct themselves, using their newly discovered ideas and vocabulary, to create pictures on stage that are designed by choice, not by chance.

SECTION I: A FINAL NOTE

I mentioned that it's imperative to begin and follow through with Section 1 before moving to other sections. It's important to understand, however, that the warm ups and exercises described do not end with these pages. They are ongoing. Students learn them, participate in them, and continue to practice them throughout the year. They are integral to everything I do in drama. They are foundational.

SECTION II:
Short Dialogues

SECTION II: FOREWARD

This section contains short dialogues, all of which are vague and open to interpretation. Students determine setting, relationship and conflict. These dialogues are great activities for introducing students (especially beginning students) to line memorization and communication of emotions, actions and pauses. You can use these dialogues in many different ways. For dialogues #1-13, I like to give each pair (or group) of students the same dialogue because it is fascinating to see and hear how their interpretations vary. Though they are all speaking the same lines, their unique choices of setting, relationship and conflict make the scenes appear fresh and different. For the dialogues where I provide the emotions (#14-46), I like to give out three different dialogues, spread out among the pairs. This format reduces the possibility of monotony. The class gets to watch, in one period, three different emotional scenes. It's important to emphasize that the emotions should be spoken exaggeratedly. This technique, if practiced repetitiously, stretches the students' emotional ranges. You will notice that some of the emotional dialogues are brief, and others are two pages long. Use accordingly, depending on the skills and abilities of your students.

DIALOGUES

Dialogue #1

#1:   Do you understand what I'm saying?
#2:   You made your point clear.
#1:   What are you going to do about it?
#2:   I have to think about it.
#1:   I will count to six.
#2:   Why not five?
#1:   I like an even number.
#2:   Well, I like odd.
#1:   I'm not surprised.
#2:   What does that mean?
#1:   One, two, three, four...

Dialogue #2

#1:   Hello.
#2:   We finally meet.
#1:   Yes, we do.
#2:   Have you considered my proposal?
#1:   I have.
#2:   And?
#1:   It is most generous of you.
#2:   Does it mean you accept the conditions?
#1:   Do you mind if I first ask you a question?
#2:   Not at all.
#1:   Have you done this before?
#2:   That I will leave to your imagination.

Dialogue #3

#1:   Hello. I was expecting you.
#2:   I'm comforted to know that.
#1:   I want this to work.
#2:   I appreciate your attitude.
#1:   But I want it to be quick.
#2:   And easy?
#1:   The easier the better.
#2:   With no regrets?

#1:	I hope not.
#2:	You don't sound sure.
#1:	Can anyone of us ever be sure?
#2:	In any case, let's proceed.

Dialogue #4

#1:	This is my favorite thing to do. How about you?
#2:	I can't say it's my favorite thing.
#1:	But you like it, nonetheless, right?
#2:	That remains to be seen.
#1:	I believe you're hurting my feelings.
#2:	I don't want to hurt your feelings, so let's proceed.
#1:	Can you at least smile or pretend to be happy?
#2:	I am here with you. Isn't that enough?
#1:	Okay, okay. I'm not going to talk about it anymore.
#2:	Good. Now are we going to start this or not?
#1:	I'm not sure I want to do it anymore.
#2:	C'mon, I thought it was your favorite thing to do.
#1:	It used to be my favorite thing, but now you've ruined it for me.
#2:	Sorry. I guess it just wasn't meant to happen.

Dialogue #5

#1:	Why are you doing this now?
#2:	Because it has to be done.
#1:	But this is not the right time.
#2:	There's no such thing as a right time.
#1:	Well, to me, there is a right time, and this is not it!
#2:	It has to be done. Just accept it.
#1:	I have plans to do something else right now.
#2:	Well, those plans will have to be put on hold.
#1:	Is it beyond you to think that I, too, might have needs?
#2:	Trust me, I have your needs in mind.
#1:	Oh really? That's a surprise to me.
#2:	If you do this with me now, there will be even more surprises for you.
#1:	I'm sorry, but this time I'm going to refuse to do what you want.
#2:	What I want is what everyone wants, including you.

#1:	Not anymore.
#2:	You will regret your decision.
#1:	Goodbye.
#2:	Goodbye.

Dialogue #6

#1:	I can't believe you're suggesting such a thing!
#2:	You're always such a baby about everything I suggest we do.
#1:	Well, this time you're really reaching outside the boundaries!
#2:	Oh, come on! Lighten up. You only live once.
#1:	And it won't be for very long if you have anything to do with it.
#2:	The real problem, my friend, is that you need to change your attitude.
#1:	No, my real problem is the friends I keep.
#2:	So now you're going to insult me because I want to bring adventure to your life?
#1:	You want to kill me. That's what you want to do!
#2:	Oh shut up already! I'm tired of your whining.
#1:	I can't believe you would talk to me that way. It's over between us.
#2:	Fine! I'll find someone else who appreciates my suggestions.
#1:	Fine!
#2:	Good riddance!

Dialogue #7

#1:	I've always wanted to do this. You know that, don't you?
#2:	I'm well aware that you've always wanted to do this.
#1:	Are you being sarcastic...because if you are...
#2:	Relax, I'm not being sarcastic!
#1:	If you don't want to do it, then at least be honest and sensitive about it.
#2:	I didn't say I didn't want to do it. You're being way too touchy.
#1:	Maybe I am being touchy. It's just that this means a lot to me.

#2:	I already said I know how much it means to you.
#1:	But you didn't say it in a voice that made me want to believe you.
#2:	Okay, what kind of voice do you want me to use?
#1:	I want you to mean what you say, that's all.
#2:	And I want you to be less touchy about everything I say or don't say.
#1:	Forget about it. I'll do it myself.
#2:	Do it yourself? Are you crazy? This is not something you can do by yourself.

Dialogue #8

#1:	So, here we are.
#2:	Yes, here we are.
#1:	Just you and me.
#2:	I've waited for this moment.
#1:	I can't say I share your feeling.
#2:	In time you may share my feeling.
#1:	Don't worry, it doesn't mean I won't do what's expected.
#2:	Do you even know what's expected?
#1:	Yes, unless you haven't been completely honest with me.
#2:	I've been as honest as I can possibly be.
#1:	That's a vague answer.
#2:	No more vague than our purpose, here and now.

Dialogue #9 (3 students)

#1:	So...
#2:	Here we are...
#3:	again...
#1:	What do you propose?
#2:	The same?
#3:	Perhaps...perhaps not.
#1:	Maybe a change?
#2:	A change?
#3:	Is it inconceivable?
#1:	Improbable.
#2:	Unlikely.
#3:	Let's give it a try.

#1:	Who put you in charge, all of a sudden?
#2:	It's not according to plan.
#3:	Sometimes plans change.
#1:	And people?
#2:	Even people?
#3:	Perhaps.
#1:	It's okay with me, if it's okay with you.
#2:	It's okay with me.
#3:	Okay, it's settled. Here we go.

Dialogue #10 (3 students)

#1:	Are you sure we can do this?
#2:	I know we can do it!
#3:	I wish I shared your optimism.
#2:	(to #3) Oh, shut up, will you? You're so pessimistic.
#3:	No, I'm just realistic.
#1:	Cool it. If we're doing this, we need to be unified.
#2:	Tell that to him/her. He/She is the problem.
#3:	Actually, the truth is, you're the problem.
#1:	Stop it, I said. Let's stay together on this.
#3:	It's okay with me, if it's okay with him/her.
#2:	(to #1) You can count on me.
#1:	Good. Let's all shake hands.
	(They shake hands.)
#1:	Okay, let's go.
#2:	Yeah, I can't wait to do this.
#3:	I'm not going. I'm sorry. (He/She leaves.)
#2:	We don't need him/her. Let's go.
#1:	Okay. (They leave.)

Dialogue #11 (3 students)

#1:	Are we ready for this?
#2:	Yes, I've been waiting all my life for this.
#3:	Hey, how about me? You haven't forgotten me, have you?
#1:	Oh, that's right. I guess we have to include you.
#2:	Do we really have to include him/her?
#3:	Thanks a lot. You really know how to make someone feel good.
#1:	If we include you, there are conditions.

#3:	Conditions? (pointing to #2) Does he/she also have conditions?
#2:	I don't need conditions.
#3:	Oh, so you're special, I guess.
#1:	Yes, he/she is special, and you're not. I can't lie.
#2:	So you see, I am special.
#3:	(To #1) How do I become special like him/her?
#1:	You follow the conditions.
#3:	And what, exactly, are these conditions?
#2:	Yeah, what are his/her conditions?
#1:	(To #2) He/She has to dance.
#3:	Dance?
#1:	(To #3) That's right. Dance.
#3:	I don't know how to dance.
#2:	Then you can't be included. (To #1) Isn't that right?
#1:	(To #2) You stay out of this. Let me make the conditions, before I make you dance as well.
#2:	Okay, no problem. I'll stay out of it.
#3:	How am I supposed to dance?
#1:	Like this. (#1 shows him/her.)
#3:	Like this? (#3 attempts to mimic #1)
#2:	(To #1) Can I do it, too?
#1:	Sure, you can do it, too. Follow me. (They all dance.)
#3:	Okay, I did it. Now am I included?
#1:	Sure, you're included. Let's go.
#2:	Hey, wait a minute. Where exactly are we going?
#3:	And what are we going to do? It's not clear.
#1:	Of course it's not clear. It's supposed to be vague?
#2/3:	Vague?
#1:	Vague!

[For Exercises #12 & #13, use one of these genres:]

Tragic Love	Action Thriller	Foreign Movie
Horror	Murder Mystery	Karate Film
Adventure	Fantasy	Heroes and Heroines
Urban Hip	Musical	Children's Story
Animation	Science Fiction	Detective Spoof
Historical	Western	Existential

Dialogue #12

#1: Now, you're absolutely sure you know what you're doing?

#2: Yes, I'm one hundred percent certain.

#1: Because if you don't you will affect a lot of people negatively.

#2: Don't worry. I'll be affecting a lot of people positively.

#1: I really hope you're right.

#2: Have you ever known me to be wrong?

#1: Well, I've known you to be a dreamer.

#2: And dreams really do come true.

#1: We're not living in a Disney movie, you know.

#2: And what I'm about to do is not make believe.

#1: If you fail, everyone you know will lose.

#2: And if I succeed, the world will forever know my name.

Dialogue #13

#1: Before we go ahead and do this, I need to know something.

#2: How can I help you, my friend?

#1: Can I trust you?

#2: After all we've been through, I'm surprised you'd ask me that.

#1: I just need some reassurance. Can you give me that?

#2: I was there for you years ago, and I'm here for you now.

#1: Thank you. I appreciate that.

#2: I'm glad. Now, are you ready to get started?

#1: Let's go before I change my mind.

#2: Here we go, once again.

Dialogue #14

     (#2 sits dejectedly)

#1: (excited) Aren't you excited to go out and start your day, live life deep and true?

#2: (crying) That's easy for you to say. You're the popular one, not me.

#1:   (angry) Oh, stop your whining and have some self-respect!

#2:   (shocked, getting up) I can't believe you're not more sympathetic to how I feel.

#1:   (laughing) You should see yourself and hear yourself. You would laugh as well.

#2:   (determined) Okay, that's it. I will show you that I also can be popular.

#1:   (fear) Did you say popular? That's impossible. Only I can be popular.

#2:   (laughing) You should see yourself and hear yourself. You would laugh as well.

#1:   (powerful) Cut it out, right now! I will make you regret ever having been born.

#2:   (paranoid) What exactly do you intend to do to me? Stay away.

#1:   (loving) Relax, I love you. Don't you know that I'm just trying to help you?

#2:   (irritated) No, I don't know that. I'm tired of your mood shifts and cruelty.

#1:   (amazed) Wow, I'm amazed at your ability to express yourself so clearly.

#2:   (confident, bold) Okay, let's go out to start our day, to live deep and true.
       (They leave.)

Dialogue #15

(#2 sits dejectedly)

#1:   (excited) I am so excited, aren't you?

#2:   (crying) You really don't know how I feel, do you?

#1:   (angry) Why do you always have to ruin everything with your crying?

#2:   (shocked) I can't believe you would talk to me in that tone of voice.

#1:   (laughing) You have no sense of humor, that's your problem.

#2:   (determined) Oh yeah, I'll show you sense of humor.

#1:   (fear) Oh no, what are you going to do?

#2:   (laughing) It's cool, don't worry. I'm only kidding.

#1:	(powerful) You better be kidding because I can crush you.
#2:	(paranoid) What exactly do you intend to do to me?
#1:	(loving) Relax, I love you. Don't you trust me?
#2:	(irritated) No, I don't. I am absolutely fed up with you. (Leaves the room.)

Dialogue #16

(#2 is lying down)

#1:	(angry) Get up! I'm not kidding this time!
#2:	(laughing) You're not kidding this time? Ha! That's funny.
#1:	(afraid) You're acting so strange, you scare me.
#2:	(powerful) I should scare you. Look what I can do.
#1:	(amazed) Wow, I've never seen anything like that!
#2:	(sickly) The problem is it's not who I really am.
#1:	(courageous) Get up now, don't let the forces of inertia defeat you.
#2:	(crying) I can't get up. I can't.
#1:	(happy) I bet I know what will get you up. This!
#2:	(irritated) How dare you insult me like that?
#1:	(loving) I wasn't insulting you. I would never do that.
#2:	(excited) I believe you. Oh yes, I do. I do!

Dialogue #17

(Both #1 and #2 are sitting, preoccupied with some activity. Then, #1 suddenly gets up.)

#1:	(paranoid) Did you hear that?
#2:	(laughing) It was nothing, just your imagination.
#1:	(angry) I hate when you say that! It's not my imagination.
#2:	(crying) Why are you yelling at me? I don't deserve that.
#1:	(pleading) Oh please don't cry. I didn't mean to yell at you.
#2:	(ambitious) Get up off your knees and stand like a man!
#1:	(amazed) Wow, I do feel like a man now.
#2:	(irritated) You are a pathetic man, that's what you

are.
#1:   (laughing) Yes I am. I know I am
#2:   (terrified) You scare me, the way your emotions change so quickly.
#1:   (powerful) Oh yeah? How about this for a changed emotion?
#2:   (loving) That's very good. I love your emotional changes.

Dialogue #18
#1:   (laughing) I can't believe we're doing this.
#2:   (angry) I wish you wouldn't be so rude about it.
#1:   (sarcastic) I'm so sorry. Am I offending you?
#2:   (crying) You really are a rotten person.
#1:   (loving) Okay, okay. I'm sorry. I really don't mean to hurt you.
#2:   (suspicious) Get away from me. I don't trust you anymore.
#1:   (crying) Please don't say that. Say you love me.
#2:   (powerful) Okay, but from now on, I'm the boss.

Dialogue #19
#1:   (amazed) Holy smoke! Look at that, will you.
#2:   (fear) I don't want to look. I'm afraid.
#1:   (courage) Don't give in to your foolish fears.
#2:   (crying) My fears are not foolish. How can you say that?
#1:   (laughing) You really are very funny, I have to say.
#2:   (angry) Shut up! Just shut up before I hit you.
#1:   (pretend fear) Oh no, I'm afraid. Don't hit me.
#2:   (laughing) Look who's the funny one now.

Dialogue #20
#1:   (angry) Get away from me. I hate you.
#2:   (loving) The more you hate me, the more I love you.
#1:   (suspicious) You really are crazy, aren't you?
#2:   (crazy) Crazy, yes! And you make me crazy—in love, that is.
#1:   (powerful) I command you to stop acting that way.
#2:   (obedient, subservient) Whatever you say. I am at

your command.

#1:   (amazed) Wow! You are the weirdest person I ever met.

#2:   (laughing) Oh, you haven't seen anything yet, believe me.

Dialogue #21

#1:   (laughing) This has to be the funniest thing I've ever seen in my life.

#2:   (angry) Have you ever considered that I don't always share your sense of humor?

#1:   (sarcastic) Oh, I guess you're just too sophisticated for me.

#2:   (crying) I can't stand you sometimes, really.

#1:   (loving) What did I do to upset you so much?

#2:   (suspicious) All of a sudden it's as if I don't know you at all.

#1:   (crying) Please tell me what it is that makes you say such things.

#2:   (powerful) I want you to leave, and I never want to see you again.

Dialogue #22

#1:   (amazed) Oh my god, I can't believe what I'm seeing.

#2:   (fear) I want to leave right now. Hurry before it's too late.

#1:   (courage) Stay where you are and rid yourself of your foolish fears.

#2:   (crying) I can't. I really can't. I must leave before I die.

#1:   (laughing) You're not going to die. You're going to live life to the fullest!

#2:   (angry) I can't stand when you don't respect what I feel.

#1:   (angry) And I can't stand when you ruin my fun all the time.

#2:   (laughing) Now you know what it's like to be me.

Dialogue #23

#1: (angry) If you do that one more time, you will be in trouble.

#2: (loving) You know that you won't really punish me.

#1: (suspicious) Get away from me. I don't trust you anymore.

#2: (crazy) I will follow you to the end of the earth, you know I will.

#1: (powerful) Get away from me right now, before I do something I regret.

#2: (obedient, subservient) Yes, yes, of course, I am here to serve you, master.

#1: (amazed) My god, you are the most insane person I have ever met.

#2: (laughing) I'll show you insane.

Dialogue #24

#1: (laughing) My gosh, you're so clumsy. You should watch where you're going.

#2: (angry) Oh shut up! Have a little sympathy, will you?

#1: (sarcastic, mimicking) Have a little sympathy, will you?

#2: (crying) I can't stand you. I don't know why I ever liked you in the first place.

#1: (loving) Oh, come on, you know exactly why you like me.

#2: (suspicious) No, I really don't know. Get away from me.

#1: (crying) Don't do this to me. Don't make me feel this way.

#2: (powerful) I can make you feel the way you make me feel.

Dialogue #25

#1: (amazed) Holy smoke! This is the greatest! The absolute greatest!

#2: (crying) I want to go home. Please take me home.

#1: (fear) Don't do that. You scare me the way you cry so suddenly.

#2:   (courage) Well, I'm not crying now, am I? Still, I want to go home.

#1:   (laughing) You're very silly sometimes. You know we can't go home right now.

#2:   (angry) I want to go home! Take me home right now!

#1:   (pleading) Okay, okay. Don't hurt me. I'll take you home right away.

#2:   (laughing) Ha-ha-ha. I'm only kidding. Can't you tell when I'm kidding?

Dialogue #26

#1:   (angry) It's over between us, and this time I'm serious!

#2:   (loving) Oh, stop it. You know you can't live without me.

#1:   (paranoid) I don't want to be near you anymore, ever again.

#2:   (crazy) Let's get one thing straight, babe. I will never leave you.

#1:   (loving) I love it when you talk to me in such a crazy way.

#2:   (amazed) Wow, you really are an emotional wreck, aren't you?

#1:   (laughing) Emotional wreck? How can you say that about the person you love?

#2:   (paranoid) Get away from me. I can't live with your emotional swings.

Dialogue #27

#1:   (sad, crying) I just can't do this anymore. I really can't.

#2:   (angry) Oh, stop acting like a baby. I'm so tired of your whining and crying.

#1:   (sarcastic, happy) Okay, I'll act happy, even though I'm really not happy.

#2:   (amazed) Wow. That was well done. You should be an actor, really.

#1:   (angry) Don't you dare make fun of me when I'm expressing real emotions.

#2: (paranoid) Real emotions? None of these emotions are real, let's be honest.

#1: (laughing) You're right, this is just an emotional exercise, isn't it?

#2: (powerful) It's an emotional exercise, but still I can overpower you, ha-ha-ha.

Dialogue #28

#1: (terrified) Don't come near me. Don't come near me. You scare me.

#2: (amazed) Wow, you really are out of sorts because of that medicine you took.

#1: (angry) I didn't take any medicine. Stop saying I took medicine.

#2: (laughing) Okay, okay. Just chill out, will you? I'm only joking.

#1: (sad, crying) You're always messing with my head. I can't take it anymore.

#2: (suspicious, paranoid) And you're making me feel very uncomfortable, really.

#1: (pleading) Oh, why can't we just get along the way we used to, please.

#2: (angry) Get along with you, you crazy loon. Stay away from me, forever!

Dialogue #29

#1: (tense) Look at me. What's wrong with me? I just can't relax.

#2: (loving) Come and sit near me. Maybe I can help you relax.

#1: (crying, hysterical) No, that won't help me. I will never relax again.

#2: (laughing) You are funny. You are so funny. You have no idea.

#1: (amazed) Wow. You really don't care how I feel, do you?

#2: (powerful, loud) I care how you feel. Do you see and hear how I care?

#1: (loving) Yes, I do see and hear how you care. Thank you so much for that.

#2:   (paranoid) Get away from me. You are the craziest person I've ever met.

Dialogue #30
#1:   (sad, crying) You don't understand what I'm saying, do you?

#2:   (angry) Maybe I would understand if you acted sane and reasonable.

#1:   (sarcastic, happy) Okay, I'll act sane and reasonable. Is this better?

#2:   (amazed) Wow. You are the most difficult person I've ever met.

#1:   (angry) And you are the most insufferable person on this planet.

#2:   (paranoid) Why do I even remain with you? What am I doing?

#1:   (laughing) Ha-ha-ha, look who's acting insane and unreasonable.

#2:   (powerful) I will make you pay for your insults and behavior.

Dialogue #31
#1:   (terrified) Oh, my god, what is that? It's the scariest thing I've ever seen.

#2:   (amazed) Wow, I think it's the most amazing thing I've ever seen.

#1:   (angry) Why don't you ever agree with me? It's scary, not amazing!

#2:   (laughing) Whoa! The only thing scary around here is you, if truth be told.

#1:   (sad, crying) You're making fun of me, and I can't stand when you do that.

#2:   (suspicious, paranoid) You're making me feel very uncomfortable right now.

#1:   (pleading) Please help me instead of making fun of me. Why can't you do that?

#2:   (angry) Get away from me, and don't ever come near me again, you crazy loon.

Dialogue #32

#1: (tense) Stop telling me to calm down. You're not feeling what I am.

#2: (loving) Relax. I'm here to help you. Take a deep breath and relax.

#1: (crying, hysterical) Relax? That's easy for you to say. I can't relax!

#2: (laughing) Okay, then stay tense for the rest of your life, I don't care.

#1: (amazed) Wow. You really are an unsenstive person, aren't you?

#2: (powerful, loud) And you are the most unrelaxed person I've ever met.

#1: (loving) Please, don't yell at me. I need love and understanding.

#2: (paranoid) Get away from me. I can't be around you anymore.

Dialogue #33

#1: (amazed) Wow, I've never seen the sky look so blue and clear!

#2: (angry) Yes you have! Yesterday the sky was blue and clear!

#1: (fear) Why are you being so mean? I was just trying to sound amazed.

#2: (mocking, mimicking, sarcastic) I was just trying to sound amazed.

#1: (laughing) Hey, that was a pretty good impersonation of me.

#2: (amazed) Wow, I'm impressed how you were able to switch emotions.

#1: (angry) You want a switch of emotions? How's this for a switch?

#2: (powerful) It's nothing like how I can switch.

#1: (crying) You always have to be better than me, don't you?

#2: (pleading) Oh, please don't cry. I was only kidding.

#1: (happy) Oh, that makes me so happy, I could cry again.

#2: (running away) You are a crazy, emotional wreck!

Dialogue #34

#1: (laughing) You are the funniest person I ever met in my life.

#2: (offended) Are you making fun of me?

#1: (angry) No, I'm complimenting you, you idiot!

#2: (crying) It doesn't sound like you're complimenting me.

#1: (loving) Look, I'm sorry. I just think that you're funny, that's all.

#2: (amazed) Really? Wow. You really think I'm funny?

#1: (paranoid) Now I'm starting to think you're crazy.

#2: (angry) I don't want to be your friend if you think I'm crazy.

#1: (crying) Please don't unfriend me. I don't have any other friends.

#2: (powerful) Stop your crying and act like a man!

#1: (powerful) Okay, do I look and sound like a man now?

#2: (laughing) No, you look and sound more like a woman.

Dialogue #35

#1: (fear) I can't do it! I can't do it! Stop asking me to do it!

#2: (loving) Relax. If you don't want to do it, then you don't have to do it.

#1: (crying, hysterical) But I have to do it. You know I have to do it.

#2: (laughing) Okay, then why don't you just do it?

#1: (amazed) Wow. That's a wonderful idea.

#2: (powerful, loud) Then go ahead and do it before I leave you alone.

#1: (loving) Please, don't leave me alone. I promise I'll do it.

#2: (paranoid) Get away from me. You're emotionally unstable.

#1: (angry) I'm supposed to be emotionally unstable. That's what the scene's about.

#2: (fear) Yes, but I'm afraid I'm not doing the scene correctly.

#1:   (happy) Just watch me. Look I'm doing it! I'm finally able to express happiness.

#2:   (amazed) Wow. I am so proud of you for finally doing it!

Dialogue #36

(#2 is lying down)

#1:   (angry) Get up, now! I'm tired of always having to be the responsible one.

#2:   (laughing) You're funny. Has anyone ever told you you're funny?

#1:   (fear) You're scaring me. I swear, you are really scaring me.

#2:   (powerful, getting up) You should be afraid. Look at what I can do.

#1:   (amazed) Wow, I had no idea you could do something like that.

#2:   (sickly) The problem is every time I do that I start to feel sick. Aaah!

#1:   (courageous) Don't give in to the sickness. You can fight it. I know you can.

#2:   (crying) I can't fight it. I can't. Every time I try to fight it, I feel worse.

#1:   (happy) I bet I know what will make you feel better. Here. Have this.

#2:   (irritated) How dare you offend me with your insulting gifts and gestures?

#1:   (loving) Oh please, don't react like that. I swear my intention was loving.

#2:   (excited) It was? I knew it! I knew it. Let's go do something exciting!

#1:   (sickly) Sorry, but all of a sudden I'm not feeling very well myself. Aaah!

#2:   (fear) Now it's you who are scaring me. I swear, you really are scaring me.

(#2 runs out of the room.)

Dialogue #37

(Both are sitting, preoccupied with some activity. Then #1 suddenly gets up.)

#1: (paranoid) Is it my imagination, or am I hearing voices in the walls?

#2: (laughing) Voices in the walls? That's the craziest thing I ever heard of.

#1: (angry) Are you saying that I'm crazy? Don't call me crazy?

#2: (crying) Don't yell at me. I wasn't calling you crazy. I wasn't, really.

#1: (pleading) Oh please don't cry. I really wish you wouldn't cry, my dear.

#2: (ambitious, getting up) Look at us! We should really stop acting so foolishly.

#1: (amazed) Wow, I like when you talk and act like that. So ambitious and bold!

#2: (irritated) You are really getting under my skin, you really are.

#1: (laughing) Oh, stop it. You know you like it when I switch emotions on you.

#2: (terrified) It worries me, though. Will we switch emotions like this forever?

#1: (powerful) It's possible. Anything's possible if you feel strong and powerful.

#2: (loving) I love it when you express yourself so strongly and powerfully.

#1: (singing) And do you love when I sing to you, as well?

#2: (paranoid) Ssh! Was that you singing, or was it a voice in the wall?
(They look at each other, and then run out of the room.)

Dialogue # 38
[The beginning emotion is angry.]

#1: Stop it!

#2: I don't want to stop it!

#1: If you don't stop, you will have consequences!

#2: Even consequences won't stop me!

(Pause. A sudden calm comes over them.)

#1: Okay, okay. Let's calm down. Deal?

#2:	Sure, I can calm down, if you can.
#1:	You've always been my favorite, you know that.
#2:	And you mine, of course.
#1:	Of course.
#2:	Yes.

(Pause. A sudden excitement strikes them.)

#1:	Then let's go out and get crazy!
#2:	Yeah, turn up, turn in, turn out!
#1:	Turn! Turn! Turn!
#2:	Every which way!
#1:	Transcend this earthly orb!
#2:	Blast ourselves into outer space!

(Pause. Suddenly sick and worried.)

#1:	Wait...I have a sudden pain in my chest.
#2:	Are you serious? That's impossible because...so do I.
#1:	What should we do?
#2:	Well, we definitely shouldn't turn up, turn in and turn out.
#1:	Definitely not.
#2:	For sure.

(Pause. Suddenly laughing.)

#1:	Hey...I think my pain has gone away.
#2:	Funny, my pain is also gone.
#1:	How strange the human body reacts and rebounds.
#2:	Yeah, it was probably just a psychosomatic reaction.

(Pause. Suddenly angry, as in the beginning.)

#1:	Why do you say that?
#2:	Why do I say what?
#1:	Are you saying my pain wasn't really real?
#2:	Whoa, you are really overreacting.
#1:	Get out! Now!
#2:	Ok, fine! This time I'm not coming back!

Dialogue #39

[The beginning emotion is excitement.]

#1:   I did it! I did it!

#2:   I am so happy for you! And for us!

#1:   Now our lives will change for the good!

#2:   No more worries about this and that.

#1:   We're going straight to the top this time!

#2:   Yes, we can finally live the dream!

(Pause. Suddenly serious and confused.)

#1:   But will we live a dream, or will it be real?

#2:   I never thought of it that way.

#1:   Something to consider, seriously.

#2:   Yes...are we awake now, or asleep?

#1:   Who can really know?

#2:   Makes you wonder, doesn't it?

(Pause. A sudden courage and determination.)

#1:   Well, whatever it is, it will be good.

#2:   That's right, even if it's a dream.

#1:   That's right, who cares if we're just imagining this?

#2:   It still feels good, that's for sure.

(Pause. A sudden loving vibe strikes them.)

#1:   Besides, what's really important is that you're with me.

#2:   By your side, as I have been, and as I always will be.

#1:   Together, through thick and thin.

#2:   Whether we lose or win.

#1:   I'm with you, and you're with me.

#2:   From sea to shining sea.

(Pause. Now an irrational fear consumes them.)

#1:   You won't ever leave me, will you?

#2:   Why do you say that?

#1:   Why don't you just say, 'No, I will never leave you!'

#2:   You're scaring me right now, the way you're talking.

#1:   I don't want to be alone, ever!

#2:   That word "alone" gives me the shivers. Don't ever speak it.

(Pause. Suddenly they laugh and become excited
again, as in the beginning.)
#1:   What are we doing?
#2:   Yeah, look at us. Two silly dillies!
#1:   What's important is that I did it!
#2:   And we're going to live the dream!
#1:   Whether we're awake or not!
#2:   O, happy illusions, forever and always!

Dialogue #40

[The beginning emotion is powerful.]
#1:   I feel so strong today.
#2:   Me too, like I can lift the world on my shoulders.
#1:   Like I can carry it around, as light as a backpack.
#2:   Like I can throw it up in the air and catch it.
#1:   Like I can crush it like a dust ball.
#2:   It's fun being strong like us, isn't it?

(Pause. A sudden fear consumes them.)
#1:   I just realized . . . someday we're going to be old.
#2:   Yeah, and we'll lose our powers.
#1:   Our muscles will turn to jello.
#2:   Someone will have to hold our spoons for us.
#1:   And feed us baby food.
#2:   Through a tube.

(Pause. Suddenly angry.)
#1:   I hate the passage of time!
#2:   It's cruel and unreasonable!
#1:   We should stay strong forever!
#2:   Yes, who's responsible for making us this way?

(Continuing with angry.)
#1:   I'd like to strangle him.
#2:   Or her.
#1:   Or her.
#2:   For playing such an ironic joke on us!

(Pause. Suddenly laughing, then calm.)

115

#1:	But let's not forget, we're only 17 right now.
#2:	That's true. Good point.
#1:	We have many years of strength ahead of us.
#2:	We're strong now, that's what's important.
#1:	Feel how strong I am.
#2:	Wow, you're really strong. And so am I!

(Pause. An excitement overwhelms them.)

#1:	Yes, let's appreciate where we are in life right now.
#2:	And live for the moment!
#1:	The beautiful here and now!
#2:	Why worry about what's ahead?
#1:	Live life to the fullest!
#2:	Young and strong!

(Pause. They begin to cry.)

#1:	Because it's not going to last.
#2:	O woe is me, to feel what I feel.
#1:	And me, too, don't forget me.
#2:	I don't want to grow old, ever!

Dialogue #41

[The beginning emotions are loving and calm.]

#1:	Isn't this just the most beautiful day?
#2:	Perfect, especially spending it with you.
#1:	I wish we could stop time right now.
#2:	And live forever in this moment.

(Pause. They look up. A sudden terror seizes them.)

#1:	Oh no! Are those rain clouds I see?
#2:	Oh, Zeus, you wicked god. Why are you doing this to us?
#1:	I don't like the feel of the wind on my skin.
#2:	(Looks down.) Oh, lordy, look! Ants are attacking us.

(Pause. They get up and move. Suddenly they feel courageous.)

#1:	Don't worry, I will save us. (Begins stepping on ants.)

#2:	And I will help you, as true as my name is Reggie! (Steps on ants as well.)
#1:	Ants and bad weather will not destroy our day.
#2:	We will prevail, though hardships come our way. (Pause. And now a sudden amazement.)
#1:	Look, the sun is coming out again.
#2:	My gosh, look at the beauty of the clouds.
#1:	Extraordinary!
#2:	Spectacular!

Dialogue #42

[The beginning emotion is courageous.]

#1:	We can do this, I know we can!
#2:	Let's remember all the training we've had.
#1:	And the fight song, remember that?
#2:	Yes, tigers, lions and bears!
#1+2:	Go! Go! Go! (Pause. They look forward, in the distance. Their emotions transition to fear.)
#1:	Oh no, all the fight songs in the world can't help us now.
#2:	And what good was all that training?
#1:	Let's face it, we are in deep trouble.
#2:	I want my mother, right now.

(Pause. They look. A sudden realization. Emotions transition to excitement and joy.)

#1:	Holy smoke! It's not what I thought.
#2:	Could it be true? We are saved!
#1:	I'll be able to get that two-car garage in the suburbs!
#2:	And a small dog named Poochie!

(Pause. A sudden emotional transition to anger.)

#1:	Did you say Poochie? Don't you know I once had a dog named Poochie that got hit by a car? (Throws #2 to the ground and walks away.)
#2:	(On the ground.) How would I know that, you crazy loon?

Dialogue #43

[The beginning emotions are upset and angry.]

#1:   Why don't you ever help me around here?

#2:   If you ask me nicely, maybe I will.

#1:   You're such a jerk, really.

#2:   And your attitude is insufferable.

(Pause. They separate. Finally they turn towards each other and transition to being suspicious and paranoid of each other.)

#1:   Who are you, anyway?

#2:   That's strange, I was thinking the same about you.

#1:   Stay clear of me, I'm serious.

#2:   Don't worry, I have no reason to go near you.
(Pause. A sudden realization. Emotional transition to amazement.)

#1:   This is amazing, truly amazing!

#2:   Yes, we've known each other for years!

#1:   And we're acting as if we're strangers to each other.

#2:   Crazy amazing, isn't it?

(Pause. The emotion transitions to happy.)

#1:   Let's celebrate our existence.

#2:   Yes, let's live deep and true.

#1:   Like there's no tomorrow!

#1:   We better stay home, where it's safe.

#2:   Yes, my love. Yes.

Dialogue #44

[The beginning emotions are determination and excitement. Play it big.]

#1:   Are you ready to do this?

#2:   I'm as ready as I'll ever be.

#1:   Then let's do it!

#2:   Yeah, let's do it!

(Pause. Emotions transition to worry and fear.)

#1:   Wait. What if we don't return?

#2:   Why are you saying that now?

#1:   I don't know, I'm just wondering...what if...

#2:   Well, I don't appreciate your...what if...

        (Pause. A sudden emotion of terror.)
#1:   Oh my god!
#2:   We're going to die, aren't we?

        (Pause. Sudden nervous laughter, increasing,
        building. Then an instant transition to seriousness
        and calm.)
#1:   We're being silly, aren't we?
#2:   Completely irrational.

        (Pause. A return to determination and excitement.)
#1:   Come on, we can do this!
#2:   For sure, let's go!

Dialogue #45

        [The beginning emotion is amazement.]
#1:   Oh my god, look at the stars!
#2:   I've never seen them so clear!
#1:   Isn't it amazing, being alone in the dark?
#2:   Absolutely, with no one around.

        (Pause. They look around. Their emotions
        transition to worry and fear.)
#1:   Wait. What was that?
#2:   What was what?
#1:   That noise.
#2:   What noise?

        (Pause. A sudden laughter consumes them. Their
        conversation becomes nervously silly sounding.)
#1:   I stepped on a twig.
#2:   Is that what the sound was?
#1:   Yes, just a silly twig snapping.
#2:   For a moment there I thought we were being
        followed by aliens.

        (Pause. They look around. They realize they are

being followed by aliens. Emotion transitions to
terror.)
#1:   Oh my god!
#2:   Run!
        (They run off.)

Dialogue #46
        [The beginning emotions are upset and angry.]
#1:   Stop chewing so loudly.
#2:   Why don't you stop shouting?
#1:   You drive me crazy.
#2:   And I hate you, I really do.

        (Pause. They separate. Finally they turn towards
        each other, transition to loving.)
#1:   I'm sorry, I love you.
#2:   And I love you, as well.
#1:   Let's never be mad at each other again.
#2:   Yes, that would make me very happy.

        (Pause. The emotion transitions to excitement.)
#1:   Hey, let's go ice skating on the frozen pond!
#2:   That's a great idea!

        (Pause. A sudden transition to fear.)
#2:   Wait. Didn't someone fall through the ice last
        week?
#1:   Oh my god, you're right!

        (Pause. The emotion transitions to loving again.)
#1:   We better stay home, where it's safe.
#2:   Yes, my love. Yes

SECTION III:
Improvisations

SECTION III: FOREWARD

I include 102 improvisations in this section. These are what I refer to as "tried and true" improvisations: those that my students have performed with confidence and success for many years. While many of the improvisations have been borrowed from other sources (books, classes and word of mouth), others I created, in collaboration with my students, through experimentation and freedom of expression. Before I list and explain the improvisations, I offer general, yet, useful notes about the performing of improvisation in a school setting. Here are some essential cardinal rules:

- Don't ask questions intended to extract exposition
- Don't deny what someone says
- Establish a character, then act as the character, not yourself
- Avoid the usual response
- Start in the middle, not the beginning.
- Assume the character, relationship and situation are already established.

When you walk in a room and see someone sitting there, assume, unless otherwise directed, you know who that person is and why that person is there.

On a related note, avoid asking questions that do little more than reflect uncertainty and insecurity. Don't ask questions just to get information (exposition) from the other person. These questions do little or nothing to enhance the improvisation or scene. Here's an example of an ineffective improvisation:

> Person A walks in the room and sees Person B.
> Person A: "Who are you?"
> Person B: "I'm your father who left you when you were a child"
> Person A: "No you're not. Who are you really? Why are you here?"

Person B: "I already told you."
Person A: "Why don't you get out now before I call the cops?"

A better choice would have been: Person A is seated; Person B walks in. Person A looks at him and says, "I was expecting you, detective.! That brings us to the next point. Don't deny what someone says. If the person walking in the room says, "Hi, Dad" don't say "I'm not your Dad." You can't kill the reality of the situation and scene. Here's another example of killing the reality of the scene by denying what the other person is saying:

A: "I want a divorce."
B: "But what about the children?"
A: "We don't have any children."

If the other person says you have children, then you have children!

Lastly, keep your improvisations fresh and original. Avoid predictable outcomes. Avoid the usual response. I'll try to demonstrate this with an extended example. Let's take the classic robbery scene. A woman comes home and finds a man stealing her possessions. Is there a typical or usual response in a situation like this? I believe so.

A: "Oh, my god!"
B: "Don't scream or I'll shoot."
A: "Take what you want, but don't hurt me."
B: "Where's your jewelry?"
A: "I don't have any jewelry."
B: "Liar! Give me your jewelry or I'll shoot."
A: "I swear I don't have jewelry."
B: "Yes you do."
A: "No I don't."
B: "Tell me or I'll shoot."
A: "Don't hurt me."

If someone were performing this improvisation, I would feel I know what they were going to say before they say it because it's the usual response. Let's take a look at a response that is not usual or typical.

> A: "Hello, am I correct in assuming that you're robbing my house?"
> B: "Yes, I am."
> A: "I don't know that I would have anything that you would want."
> B: "Well, these paintings are exquisite! I can tell they're not originals, but they are worth something."
> A: "Thank you, I painted those."
> B: "What? I am impressed. This one, in particular, is incredible work!"
> A: "I am flattered. I insist you have it."
> B: "I'd feel uncomfortable taking your best work."
> A: "But I insist."
> B: "I want you to know I appreciate your generosity."
> A: "And I appreciate your appreciation of my art. No one has ever told me I was a good artist."
> B: "That's hard for me to believe."
> A: "Well, it's true."
> B: "You know, after I'm finished here—robbing you—if you're interested we could go for a cup of coffee or a bite to eat. I know I'm a robber, but I'm also a pretty nice guy."
> A: "I would love to."
> B: "Great, well, I suppose I should go on with my business here."
> A: "Yes, you should. Don't mind me if I'm in the other room."
> B: "I undid your closet, if you don't mind me saying so."
> A: "I appreciate your telling me."
> B: "I'll just let myself out when I'm finished, is that okay?"
> A: "Yes."
> B: "Great, I'll call you later."

Because the above improvisation has an unusual response, it is fresh and unpredictable. It also moves forward towards a resolution. And this brings me to my next point: While conflict is an essential part of human relationships and situational scenes, it doesn't always play well on stage if all it does is turn into an endless argument (such as the typical robbery scene). Sometimes agreeing is more interesting because as well as being more unusual it moves a scene forward.

Here are Some Additional Notes to Consider:

1. Improvisations take place in the "now" (the present). Pay attention and listen. React not as you think you should but in a way that is fresh and unusual.

2. Improvisations should be short and quick. Establish your character, your relationship to the other person, what you want in the situation, and then move towards a resolution.

You should end them on your own in a clean, satisfying fashion. Avoid bailing out at the end because you don't know what else to say or do.

3. Use your imagination and react as the character in the situation would react. You're not playing yourself. You're not in the situation. The character is in the situation. Don't resist due to self-consciousness.

4. An improvisation—just like a scene—is not a verbal race from beginning to end. The nonverbal component is just as important. Sometimes we stare with disbelief at someone after he says or does something. Sometimes we walk away. Sometimes we laugh. Sometimes we cry. Sometimes we sit back, take out a stick of gum and chew it, while crossing our legs. IN OTHER WORDS, WE DO THINGS! A pause in speaking allows the audience to digest, absorb, interpret, and appreciate.

5. Always stay within the context of the situation. Be true to your character, the relationship, the situa-

tion. Avoid stepping "outside" just for the sake of shock value or a cheap laugh. Humor is best when it comes naturally from truthful situations.

6. Avoid profanity and vulgar references. They do little more than embarrass your audience. Discretion is a necessary part of the creative process.

Okay, now here are the 102 improvisations I promised. Keep in mind that describing an improvisation is nearly impossible. Many variations and interpretations exist. What I offer are the bare bones. Find the flesh of these improvisations by doing them with your students and modify accordingly, on your terms, in whatever way suits the needs of both you and your students. The order of the improvisations here in no way suggests a sequence. They are mostly independent of one another. Pick and choose as you please.

IMPROVISATIONS

1. House Improvisation

I created this high-speed, rapid-movement improvisation with my students many years ago. Somehow the name "House" stuck because the set up for the improvisation is a house, with couch, chair, table, telephone, etc. This one can last anywhere from 5 to 50 minutes, depending on the ideas and creativity of the group. Here's the format: One student (the main person) is on stage the entire scene. The scene begins with this person walking on stage and showing her state of mind, through actions and behaviorisms, given the situation or problem she is given. Here's a situation I might give: "You enter your house after walking home, believing that someone is following you." Next come telephone calls, one at a time, from anyone in the class. These calls should further instigate or complicate the main person's problem. Telephone calls should be made throughout the scene. As well as making calls, anyone can enter the scene and interact with the main person. He should make his visit brief, however. No more than two students, including the main person, should be on stage at one time. It's important that this scene moves quickly from telephone calls to visits. No call or visit should last more than 20-30 seconds.

Here are some suggestions for problems or situations:

1. Someone is following you.
2. You witnessed a crime.
3. It's your birthday yet no one acknowledged it.
4. You found a suitcase full of money.
5. You just got fired from your job.
6. You were driving home from work; you ran over your neighbor's dog.
7. You just came back from the doctor; you received bad news.
8. You received a bad haircut.
9. Your car broke down; you are forced to stay at a

strange motel.

10. You just got home from school; no one asked you to the prom.

2. Six Characteristics

This one is an improvisation for two performers. The pair is given a situation, and they must perform a 1-minute improvisation in which they include six characteristics, in any order they choose, such as the following:

- A laugh of some kind
- A sigh
- A snap of fingers
- An exclamation
- A threat
- A line from a song or poem

I keep the situations simple. Here are some examples:
1. First date issue
2. Waiter/customer problem
3. Teacher/student conflict
4. Romance breakup
5. Someone owes money
6. Friends uncertain about future plans
7. Army personnel disagreement
8. Social media conflict
9. Mother/daughter issue over chores
10. Parent-child expectations

3. Eight Characteristics

This one is the same as Six Characteristics, except the students must include the following eight characteristics, in any order they choose, in a one-minute improvisation:

- crying
- an animal sound
- rubbing of hands

- a literary allusion
- a whistle
- tying of a shoe
- the words "That's sexy"
- a handshake

4. Two-Minute Drill News Program

Place a small table and chair center stage. To the left and right place a pair of chairs, making five total chairs. This one is a rapid-fire improvisation, where five students perform a news program containing 15 stories. The person sitting behind the center table controls the speed and flow of the improvisation. He is the newscaster. The others are his news associates, acting as reporters, interviewers and anyone else who is necessary to convey the news stories. Though this one is a rapid-fire improvisation, the stories must be compelling and comprehensible.

5. Sentence Repeat 30 Seconds

Two performers sit side by side. They are given a sentence. In 30 seconds, they must repeat this sentence, alternating from one performer to the other, as quickly and comprehensibly as possible, each time using their voices differently, so that no two repeats sound alike. Here are some sentences I use:

1. This is the craziest thing I've ever seen in my life.
2. This is the most unbelievable day of my life.
3. Today I will not allow myself to be pushed around.
4. All we ever do is say the same thing over and over.
5. Do you think we'll get out of here alive?
6. I absolutely hate it when you repeat yourself.
7. Look at the size of the ocean wave coming towards us.
8. It's going to be summer soon, I can feel it.
9. This has to be the worst movie ever made.
10. This is not going to be easy, but we can do it.

6. Using the Same Sentence Often

I give a sentence to three students. Their task is to perform an improvisation no longer than 1 minute. They are not limited to speaking only this sentence. They can use as many words and sentences as they like. But, during the scene each student must use the sentence as many times as possible. Each time they use it, they should vary their voices and tones. Here are some sentences I use:

1. Can it get any more absurd?
2. This is not getting us anywhere.
3. This is not what's supposed to happen.
4. I think you're crazy, that's what I think.
5. This is absolutely unbelievable.
6. Oh boy, here we go again.
7. I'm starting to understand what you're saying.
8. Is this a dream, or is it real?
9. I think we're finally getting somewhere.

7. Using the Same Word Often

Similar to using the same sentence often, this one varies slightly. This time three students perform a 1 minute improvisation, using a single word (or any variation of its form) often. For example, if I give the word "Temptation," the students will use this word as much as possible in their scene. They can also use the word "Tempting," since it's a variation of "Temptation." The entire improvisation revolves around this word and its implied and literal meanings. Here are a list of words I like to use with this one:

1. Temptation
2. Compassion
3. Unsolvable
4. Corruption
5. Jealousy
6. Problematic
7. Morality
8. Frustration
9. Scandalous
10. Irreplaceable

8. Adding Nouns

This improvisation has no time limit. It can last as long as the performers' verbal and creative stamina. Two students stand or sit on stage. The improvisation begins with a noun. I say, "Clock." The students create a scene, focusing on this word. I quickly add a second noun, such as "Sweater." The students now focus on "Sweater," while continuing to integrate the first word "Clock." I continue to add words, and they continue to integrate each new noun and all the nouns that precede it. What makes the improvisation challenging and especially fun to watch is that the nouns have no apparent relationship to one another. In a typical improvisation, I might call out as many as 15 words. Here are some examples:

Telephone	Tree	Harmonica
Chair	Shaving cream	Hammer
Princess	Lettuce	Butterfly
Magazine	Chewing gum	Tiger
Football	Hamburger	Shoelace

9. Piano Pantomimes

If you have a room with a piano (and a student who can play it), this is an improvisation that is quick, easy and fun to watch. The piano player plays something dramatic. Two students perform a 20-second scene, establishing setting, relationship, and story, emphasizing their facial expressions and actions.

10. Piano Musicals

This improvisation can include 2-5 students. The piano plays, changing tunes every ten seconds or thereabouts. The students on stage create a scene, suggested by the audience, singing their lines, coordinating their voices with the tone and style of the music playing.

11. The Reverse

I have two students perform an ending dramatic moment, lasting no more than 10 seconds. I then instruct them to go backwards in the scene, to the previous 45 seconds, leading up to the ending scene. They perform the entire scene, including, once again, the dramatic ending.

12. Closing Line

I give two students a closing line. They tell the class the last line, and then they perform a 45 second improvisation that ends naturally on the closing line. Here are some closing lines I use:

1. Didn't your mother ever tell you not to play with fire?
2. As you see, dreams sometimes do come true.
3. I guess you're not such a big shot anymore, huh?
4. Before you leave, let me say this: good luck, my friend.
5. You blew your one chance at stardom, buddy.
6. I'm letting you go, even though I don't believe you.
7. I told you from the start you were fighting a losing battle.
8. Before you walk out that door, understand this: I love you.
9. I will never forget what you did for me.
10. Next time you have an impulse to run away, consider the consequences.

13. World Famous Therapist

This therapist is so famous that he or she can only take one new patient. 10-15 students audition to be that one lucky patient. The therapist sits behind a small table. Each prospective patient appears on stage and has 15 seconds to communicate his unique problem to the therapist. If a door is available, have all the students come from this door. Otherwise, they can just stand in a line and enter one at a time. After each student has presented his unique problem, the therapist asks the audience to help decide which patient he or she will accept as a patient.

14. Three Tables Related Stories

Three pairs of students sit at three different tables. The right table pair establishes their characters. When I say "Switch," the improvisation moves to the center table pair. They begin their scene, finding a way to incorporate the first pair into their scene, through their relationship to one another. When I say "Switch" again, the improvisation moves to the left table pair. They find ways to relate their characters and scene to the previous ones. Therefore, though there are three tables, each with different characters and situations, the collective scene shows their relationships to each other. This improvisation can continue for as long as the students have ideas.

15. Outrageous Late-for-School Excuses

While this one shares similarities with the give-me-the-chair improvisation, the format is very different. For this one, I simulate a classroom environment, setting up a table and 6-8 chairs, diagonal to the table. I have a student play the teacher, sitting at the table. 10-12 students line up and come in one at a time, each one with an excuse why he was late. If his reason is clever and witty and imaginative, he is told by the teacher to take a seat. If the teacher doesn't like the excuse because it is either cliché or ordinary, he will tell the student to go to the office to get a pass. This one, like give me the chair, is either win or lose. You either sit (win) or you go to the office (lose). One of the important differences with this one is that the teacher is the one who decides. Therefore, it's recommended that you choose one of your better improvisational students, someone who can make fair determinations, which are neither too hard nor too easy. The improvisation ends when all the seats in the classroom are occupied. Of course, if no one wins a seat in the classroom, you will have to use your judgment when to end the improvisation.

16. Classroom Experts

I simulate a classroom environment, setting up a table and 8-10 chairs, diagonal to the table. One student plays the teacher, sitting at the table. On the floor in the center of the room are 10-12 props. 8-10 students enter the classroom one at a time, greeting the teacher and taking a seat. When everyone is seated, the teacher calls on a specific student to stand front and center. The teacher then selects a prop, hands it to the student, and tells the audience that this particular student is an expert historian on the artifact (prop) he is holding. The student speaks scholastically about the prop, sounding professorial. The teacher and audience members ask questions to the expert. The improvisation continues until all the students in the simulated classroom have had a chance to speak expertly about a prop.

17. Classroom Emotions

The set up is the same as Classroom Experts, except this one does not involve props. Each student entering the classroom is given an emotion. Each student must act his emotion the entire improvisation. As each student enters the classroom, he interacts with the teacher, expressing his specific emotion. When all the students have entered the classroom, the teacher will call on a student to stand front and center. The teacher will ask this student questions. This improvisation asks the audience members to participate. Each "emotion" student on stage has a parallel "emotion" parent in the audience. The parent, at any time, can call or visit the student. The parent expresses the same emotion. The improvisation ends when each of the parents comes to the classroom, one at a time, to pick up his child from school.

18. Classroom Genres

This one is very similar to Classroom Emotions, except I substitute emotions for genres. Each student is given a genre to play, and each student has a parallel genre parent in the audience.

19. Customer Service Return

You will need a great many props or objects for this one. A customer service person stands behind a table. 10-12 students form a line and enter one at a time. Each of these students tries to return an object (prop). The customer service person makes it difficult for the customers. In fact, he should not accept any returns. His job is to make quick work of the customers, no matter what they say. Unlike the previous two improvisations, the customers cannot win. What makes this one appealing is that the customers are up against the iron will and nasty personality of the customer service person. You will, of course, need a student who can play this customer service person with a combination of wit, charm and comic nastiness. No matter what the customers say, no matter how good their reasons are for returning or exchanging their objects, the customer service person should, nonetheless, send each one on his way, quickly.

20. Ending Photograph

Two students stand on stage. I have someone from the audience create an intriguing photograph with the two students. The sculptor shapes the two students' arms, legs, head, posture, etc. It's important that the photograph suggest a relationship of some form between the two students. Otherwise, the photograph can be somewhat outrageous. Once the photograph is established, I tell the two students on stage that this pose they're in is the final image of their scene. They go off stage. When they enter from opposite sides they have one minute to begin an improvisation, ending in the final photograph.

21. The Magic Prop

I place a box of props on stage. Two students come on

stage. They are given a random prop. They must create a one-minute improvisation, creating a setting, story and characters, in which the prop in their possession has magical properties.

22. First Two Lines

Two students are given the first two lines of a scene/story. They must instantly decide who they are, where they are, and what is happening. The improvisation should be no longer than one-minute. Here are a few examples:

> #1: Make me an offer.
> #2 Okay, here it is.

> #1: Don't you dare do that.
> #2: It'll be okay, don't worry.

> #1: Hurry up, we're wasting time.
> #2: Don't rush me, I don't want to mess up.

> #1: Look who's laughing now, huh?
> #2: Oh shut up, at least I tried.

23. First Three Lines

The only difference between this one and "First Two Lines" is that this one uses three students. Here are some examples:

> #1: Where is it?
> #2: I don't know, I thought you had it.
> #3: Are you knuckleheads trying to tell me you lost it?

> #1: Are you ready for this?
> #2: I'm as ready as I'll ever be.
> #3: I'm feeling sick, if you want to know the truth.

24. Three Emotions

Two students are given three emotions. They must create a one-minute improvisational scene, with setting, relationship, character and conflict. The scene must follow the order of the emotions, switching from one to the next every twenty seconds. Here are a few examples:

1. Angry, laughing, afraid
2. Amazed, crying, powerful
3. Apologetic, irritated, enthusiastic

25. Make a Drawing

On a sheet of paper, two students make an abstract drawing. These drawings then get passed around. When each pair has a drawing made by a different pair, the improvisations begin. Two students stand front and center. They show their drawing to the audience. They then have 30-45 seconds to act out their interpretation of the drawing.

26. Emotion and Location

I always keep a stack of index cards with me. Some have emotions written on them, and others have locations written on them. In this improvisation, two students pick first an emotion card and then a location card. They then perform a 30-45 second improvisation, creating relationship and story. Here are some examples:

1. Crying, Christmas morning
2. Frustrated, hiking trail
3. Excited, science lab
4. Terrified, school cafeteria
5. Amazed, outer space

27. Jake and Jim

I select two students to play Jake and Jim. They stand to

the side, either right or left. Another student, someone who is very good at pantomime, sits or stands in the center. This person will take her cues from Jake and Jim. Jake and Jim announce an ordinary event, such as eating cereal or tying a shoe or brushing teeth. But they announce this ordinary activity as if it were the greatest event ever taken place. They will play off each other and use exclamations such as "Oh, my god, Jim, did you see the way she put that toothpaste on her brush." "I swear to god, Jake, I've never seen anyone squeeze a tube of toothpaste like that before. Let's see a replay on that." This is a hilarious improvisation if you can find the right students to perform it. Jake and Jim should have no limitations on their exclamations and their insistence on rewinding or fast forwarding. The student performing the pantomime must be courageous and completely in the moment, willing to do whatever Jake and Jim say. I'm sure this improvisation, in other circles, has another name. I call it Jake and Jim because when I was young I had imaginary announcers in my head called Jake and Jim.

28. Judgment Day

This one belongs in the category of storytelling. I choose five students and have them sit in chairs, facing the audience. Each student is given a character. I always keep a folder with the names of characters written on pieces of paper. Each of the students (characters) is instructed to tell a story independent of one another. The basketball coach has his own story; the librarian has her own story; the hot dog vendor has his own story, and so on. I use a tapper, who stands behind the students. When he taps a student, it signals the student to speak. On the second tap, the student stops speaking. He then taps someone else, and the process continues. The reason for the tapper is this: I want the stories to be serial, not continuous from beginning to end. I want to see and hear the student's story in 15-second installments.

Here's the way it's designed to work: the tapper taps the basketball coach. He begins his story. When he is tapped again, he stops, in mid sentence, perhaps. The tapper taps the librarian. She begins her story. When she is tapped a second time, she stops. The tapper then taps the other characters, signaling them when to begin and when to stop. There is no specific sequence for the tapper. He can select whomever he wants to tap, in any order. When he re-taps the basketball coach, or any of the characters, the student assuming the character continues where he left off, in mid sentence. Typically, students are tapped four or five times in one improvisational activity. I usually signal when they should end their story. I will say, "Okay, this is the last time you're tapped, so wrap it up." As for the improvisation itself, here's the reason I call it Judgement Day instead of standard Storytelling: the characters in the chairs are all condemned to hell. They have done something bad in their lives, but they have a chance to explain to the audience, which acts as a jury, that they were justified in doing what they did. I tell both the students telling the story and those listening that if the stories are imaginative and clever, if the characters are well delivered, meaning their voices and their physical characteristics, then the jury should pardon them. At the end of the activity, when the stories are finished, the class votes—thumbs up or down—for each storyteller. "Should he be saved or not?" That's the question I ask to the jury, while standing behind each character, one at a time.

It's important that the storytellers know they are going to have four or five turns at speaking. This way they can pace their story. Ideally, they should build their story, so that the second time they are tapped, and each subsequent time, they are adding more interesting detail. They want to save their culminating detail for the end, when they make their final plea to the audience.

29. Pantomimes to Music

This one is a favorite of mine. A student brings in his i-pod or laptop, something that contains a large collection of music. It's best if the music doesn't have words. Classical music and sound track music work best. We plug the i-pod into a speaker and we're ready to begin. In this improvisation, music plays and students, in pairs, create a story without words, using what they've learned of pantomime and nonverbal expression. As the music changes, the story changes. I like to do this improvisation with my entire class, and this is how I format it: I assign everyone a partner. I have half the students sit downstage, while the other half stands in the wings: one partner in the left wing, one in the right. When the music begins, the pairs, one at a time, enter from different sides. Their job is to create a story, nonverbally. What's important, I tell them, is to establish setting, character and relationship. They must allow the music to dictate and shape their decisions. Each pair is allowed 15-20 seconds; therefore, they can't wait too long. They need to make a decision soon after the music starts. This exercise forces them to work together, not individually. One of them will have to relent to the other since it's unlikely that each is going to make a choice at the same time. To administer this improvisation smoothly and efficiently, I assign each pair a number before we begin. Each number corresponds with a new piece of music. When I say, "Number One," the first piece of music begins, and the #1 pair comes on stage. When I say "Number Two," a new track plays, and the #2 pair enters. The #1 pair leaves and join the students in the audience.

The improvisation should be as continuous and seamless as possible, with little lag time between new music and new pairs. Sometimes I vary the format. If I have two extremely talented pantomime performers, I may keep them on stage as the music changes, forcing this pair to tell new stories approximately every 20 seconds. Whatever format is used, whether it's rotating students or keeping the same pair on stage, this improvisation brings together music, pantomime, movement and scene building in exciting, entertaining ways.

30. Music Stories

This improvisation also involves music, but this time someone is playing a guitar. I have five students stand on stage.

I tell the guitar player to change the tone and mood every 15 seconds. One at a time, the speakers tell a continuous story, using the guitar music as an influence. The speakers change, the music changes, the story changes. This improvisation is a marriage between music and story. Speakers must coordinate their story with what they hear, how fast or slow, the mood and tone sounds to them.

31. Songs with Themes

Similar to the previous one, the students this time create a song, one sentence at a time. The guitar player doesn't switch his rhythm and tone as much in this improvisation. I don't want the students who are singing to be confused. After all, it's hard enough to make up words and to sing in front of others. In fact, only the most natural singers or most daring students will want to attempt this one. Often I have someone from the audience suggest a theme before we begin, though this feature is not necessary.

32. Single Prop Never Before Seen

Two students lie on stage, on opposite sides, suggesting sleep. Between them is placed a prop. When they open their eyes, they recognize each other, but they have never before encountered the prop. Their confusion of this prop initiates the scene. It doesn't matter the size and shape of the prop. The students must be baffled by its existence. They may even be terrified by it. They should move around it with trepidation. The strangeness of the prop should also affect their relationship with one another. It's as if the object were placed there to disturb their lives. To add an entertaining element I usually, at some point—perhaps 30-45 seconds into the improvisation—have a student in the audience assume the voice of the prop. It can be very humorous to have two students baffled by a prop, maybe even afraid of it, and then be ordered and controlled by it. For example, if the prop is a sombrero, the voice at one point might say, "Lift me up. Now place me on your friend's head. Now I want you to say to your friend, 'You look stupid.' I admit, this is a very strange improvisation, but I guarantee it's funny when the prop has a higher status than the players involved in the scene.

33. Trying to Win the Hand of the Prince/Princess

I place two students on stage. One is the King and the other is the Princess. This is the day the King is offering his daughter's hand to suitors from beyond the kingdom. Each suitor brings a gift (a prop) and a creative reason why he should marry the Princess. In this improvisation, the King should be hard to please. I usually have 10-12 students, all equipped with props of various sizes and shapes, lined up ready to enter the scene. One at a time, the suitors enter, make their offer and are quickly sent on their way. Even if the King were to like one of the suitors, the Princess should find a reason to reject the person. The King says, "Leave at once" and then "Next," signaling the following suitor. I also have students perform this improvisation starting with a Queen and a Prince. In this format, girls will become the suitors. If you use both formats, you will ensure that you are involving an equal number of males and females.

34. Mannerism Interviews

One student is interviewing the other. I don't specify the nature of the interview. It could be for a job. It could be to join a club. It could be a news-related interview. Each student is given a mannerism, a defining characteristic to use at their discretion, though not continuously or repetitive, without purpose. This mannerism influences each student's behavior, determining their relationship to one another and the tone and direction of the scene. Here's a listing of some mannerisms I give to my students:

Whistle	Sigh	Giggle
Crack knuckles	Rub face	Sway/rock
Clear throat	Rub eyes	Sniff
Touch lips	Rub temple	Rub chin
Scratch head	Rub hands	Touch nostrils

35. Interview with Seven Characteristics

This one-minute interview improvisation for two students must include these characteristics in this order:

- vigorous handshake
- shared laugh/excitement over a common interest
- a sudden disagreement, turned shouting match
- one person pacing around the room
- one person apologizing
- a shared, meditative, relaxed moment
- a decision whether to hire the person or not

36. Subconscious

This improvisation involves four students and follows a strict order. Two students sit down and converse, while two students stand behind each one, acting as his subconscious. Let's say that a boy and girl are on a first date. Behind the boy stands another boy, acting as his subconscious. Behind the girl stands another girl acting as her subconscious. Here's the order:

- The boy seated speaks first
- His subconscious speaks next
- The girl seated speaks
- The girl's subconscious speaks

This order repeats itself as long as the improvisation moves along creatively and cleverly. In order for the improvisation to be effective, the player's must follow specific rules of the improvisation. First, the people seated only hear each other. They cannot react to anything the subconscious characters are saying because they don't really hear them. It is the job of the subconscious characters to create the necessary irony that takes place between what one says and what one is really thinking. The subconscious characters do hear each other and must do all they can to sustain the irony and, thus, humor. The following is an example of how this improvisation might begin:

> *Boy: I'm having a great time.*
> *His Subconscious: This is about as much fun as doing math homework.*
> *Girl: Me too.*
> *Her Subconscious: Oh, I want to marry him. I know he's the one for me.*
> *Boy: You have a nice smile.*
> *His Subconscious: My gosh, if I had teeth like hers I would never smile.*
> *Girl: Thank you.*
> *Her Subconscious: He loves me, I know it. The last guy I dated made fun of my teeth.*

As you can see, the introduction to this improvisation has the necessary irony to make it humorous. The students playing the subconscious characters need to be some of your most clever students. The wit, irony and humor are dependent on their ability to sense what the improvisation needs at any given moment.

37. Storytelling Vowels

A couple of different formats can be used for this improvisation. The one I favor uses three tables, two chairs at each. I give each pair of students a vowel. They must converse with one another, one at a time, emphasizing the vowel sound. In other words, if the first pair is given the vowel O, they must exaggerate this sound as much as possible. It doesn't mean that everything they say has an O sound, but it should be clear that they are emphasizing this vowel. I let this pair speak for 15-20 seconds. When I say "Next" the second pair begins their conversation, emphasizing the vowel A. After 20 seconds, I signal the next pair, emphasizing the E sound, to begin. When I return to the first pair, they continue where they left off. Then the second and third pairs continue accordingly. Another format I use is as follows: I have five students sit in chairs facing the audience. I tell the students they will tell a story, emphasizing whatever vowel I happen to call out. In this format, the story they tell is continuous. What changes is the emphasis of the vowel. This one is more challenging than the first format because the students need to pay attention to the story that is being told, and they need to switch their vowel emphasis suddenly and often.

38. Storytelling Consonants

The format and guidelines for this improvisation are nearly the same as the vowels. The only change is that instead of vowels the students are given consonants to emphasize. Therefore, instead of A, E, I, O, U, the emphasis will be on consonants such as B, D, K, P, and T. Of course, these are not the only consonants, but I tend to favor these.

39. Storytelling Patterns

While this improvisation can be done in a large group, in a circle either standing or sitting, I prefer using a storytelling format, with five students sitting in chairs facing the audience. The students tell a continuous story, one that adheres to the word pattern I give them. For instance, I might tell them to follow a 1, 2, 3 pattern. It's very important that they follow the order I detail below. Here's what it would look like if five students were following this pattern:

> #1: *The*
> #2: *sun was*
> #3: *shining in the*
> #4: *sky*
> #5: *on that*
> #1: *day in October.*
> #2: *My*
> #3: *eyes were*
> #4: *distracted by the*
> #5: *blinding*
> #1: *light that*
> #2: *reflected from the*

#3: windows
#4: on the
#5: car in front
#1: of
#2: me. I
#3: couldn't see, but...

As you can see, if I use five students it ensures that they will be alternating how many words they speak. This pattern is, of course, only one of dozens I can use. I do, however, attempt to keep the patterns simple. I very rarely go past four words at one time. If the students are confused and begin counting numbers on their fingers it will not be an effective improvisation. Ideally, this improvisation should be performed fluently, with little hesitation, as if it were being spoken by one voice.

40. Two-Person Gibberish Translations

Two pairs of students sit at tables, left and right. I direct the two students who are sitting stage left to perform a 20-second scene, with demonstrable emotions and actions. In this scene, however, they are not speaking English. They are speaking gibberish. The students who are sitting stage right must translate the gibberish scene into English. When their translation is complete, they then perform their own 20- second gibberish scene, in which case the other pair becomes the translators.

41. Three Tables Gibberish Translation

This format offers variation to the previous one. It involves six students, pairs sitting at three tables, and it lasts much longer. The left table pair performs a 20-second gibberish scene. The center table translates it into English. Then the right table pair performs a gibberish scene. This time the left table translates it into English. The center table pair then perform a gibberish scene that the right table pair translates into English. This improvisation has no time limit. It can continue as long as the six students want.

147

42. Alphabet Improvisation

This one can also take on many different shapes and forms. The key element is that students have to tell a story in the sequence of the alphabet. For instance, if two students are standing or sitting on stage, one must begin the scene, using a sentence beginning with the letter "a". The other student continues their scene, starting his sentence with the letter "b". The object for the students is to make it all the way to Z. This one has rules. First of all, students must speak sensible, grammatical sentences. Second, they must continue a sensible, coherent story. And lastly, they must speak fluently, without stalling and counting on their fingers for the next alphabet word. In other words, the improvisation must look and sound natural. It's like any scene, except in this one they must know their alphabet and be clever enough to tell a continuous story in a proper alphabet sequence. While the above example involves two students, I often use the storytelling format I use with many of the preceding improvisations. I have five students tell a continuous story, one sentence (letter) at a time. Here they're not interacting the way two students are. They are instead telling a story. The rules, of course, are the same whether you use two students in a scene or five students in a storytelling format.

43. Alphabet Line

This one is a variation to the alphabet format involving five students sitting in chairs. In this one, I have as many as ten students stand in a line. They tell a continuous story, following the sequence of the alphabet.

44. Rhyme Improvisation

The format for rhyme is similar to the alphabet improvisation. I can use two students in an interactive scene or five students telling a story. What's important here is that their sentences rhyme. For the sake of simplicity and clarity, I tell students to use couplets. One student says a sentence.

The next student completes the rhyme. In other words, someone says, "Do you want to take a walk today?" The other student—if it's a two-person format—says, "I'd rather wait till the month of May." If two students are engaged in this improvisation, they must vary their pattern so that the second student is not the one who is always completing the rhyme. If you use a two-person format, the second student should not only complete the rhyme, but he should then start the following sentence. For instance, he says, "I'd rather wait for the month of May" followed by "because right now I have a bad back." Then the first student has to rhyme with the word "back". If you're using a storytelling format with five students, I recommend the following format: the students tell a continuous story, one sentence at a time. The first student starts the story with a sentence. The second student completes the rhyme. The third student continues the story, but since the preceding rhyme has been completed he doesn't have to continue with the same sound. If the first two sentences end with the sound A, he can say a sentence ending with the sound E. The fourth student completes his rhyme. After the fifth student says his sentence, the order goes back to the first student. This pattern assures that the students are sometimes completing the rhyme and sometimes starting it. The challenge here is that the story must make sense, albeit in rhyme. It should also be done fluently without stalling and stopping. The improvisation ends when the students fail to continue either the rhyme or the story.

45. Rhyme Line

In this improvisation, I have ten students stand in a line. I give them a sound, such as "O" and tell them to tell a story or poem that uses the "O" sound. Each student speaks a sentence that ends in the sound.

46. Environmental Switches

I use 5 students for this improvisation. I make available on the stage several chairs and tables for their use, if needed.

As this one states in the title, the environment switches. How many switches and how often is up to the discretion of the teacher. Generally, if an improvisation moment is electric I let it play out. If the vibe isn't there, I switch quickly. I keep my eyes and ears open to what's happening on stage. The students I choose for this one must be playful, spontaneous and daring. I start by calling out an environment: "Locker room after a tough loss." I count to eight, giving the students time to assemble themselves and make quick decisions about who's the coach, the players, etc. Also, if they need chairs or tables they can move them into position. On average, each environment improvisation might last 20 seconds, at which time I'll call out another environment. This is a fast-moving improvisation. Students shift situations, characters and relationships. I like to give the students unusual environments, those that will challenge their imaginations. Here's a sampling of switches I might use:

1. Deep Sea Divers
2. Trenches World War I
3. Café Poetry Open Mic
4. Someone's 5th Birthday Party
5. Aliens Landing on Earth, Meeting Humans
6. Immigrants Learning English
7. Birthing Class for Couples
8. Cave Men Performing a Wedding
9. Criminal Trial Case
10. Bank Robber

47. Car Mimic

I place four chairs on stage, staggering two in front and two behind, simulating the seating positions in a car. The improvisation starts with one person sitting in the driver's seat. Two others sit in the back seat. 10-12 students, or more, form a line adjacent to the chairs. When I say "Next" the first student in line occupies the empty passenger seat. This student enters the car with a very specific character voice and repetitive mannerism. The other students in the car must mimic him, moving as he does, speaking as he does. To be effective in this improvisation, the lead student must not do too much. He has to keep his actions simple and repetitive, allowing the other students to mimic him without much difficulty. If the lead student moves too much and speaks uncontrollably, the other students will have little chance mimicking him. This one is also a fast-moving improvisation, and it's ideal if you want to use the entire class. I usually rotate my students. I'll have half of them do the improvisation, and then when this half is finished, I'll have to other half give it a try. The challenge is to try to get everyone in the car, all four students, doing the same thing, at the same time, speaking in the same tone of voice. The others in the car do not have to say exactly what the lead character is saying, but they have to be the same character, with the same actions. You want this one to move along quickly. I'll typically say "Next" every 10-15 seconds. Again, as with the previous improvisation, I take my cue from the students. If the students on stage are aligned and in sync, I'll let them continue longer. Conversely, if the students are not watching and listening to the lead character, or if the lead character doesn't follow the rules well enough, I move to the next person.

48. Shared Mannerisms in a Revolving Scene

This improvisation shares some similarities with the "Car Mimic" but whereas the former improvisation is largely a mimic exercise involving four people, this one is a two-person, scene-related improvisation. One person is already seated on stage. Someone enters with a definitive manner-ism and a specific voice. The person in the room must assume the same features, but they are not mimicking what each other says. They are engaged in a dialogue. They just happen to have the same mannerism and voice texture. When I say "Next" the first student leaves and a new student enters. He will bring in his own unique mannerism and voice quality. The student left on stage must now adapt to this new person and assume new characteristics. Typically, I will have 10-12 students waiting in the wings, ready to enter. This is why I call it a revolving scene. Someone is always leaving and someone is always entering.

49. Freeze Tag

I use several variations of freeze tag. Sometimes I limit it to two people on stage. Other times I add a third, fourth and fifth person. Let me start with the simplest form, using two people. To start, I have two students enter from opposite sides of the stage. I give them a situation, anything to get the improvisation started. I might say, "One of you is the karate master, the other is his pupil." The students will quickly engage in an activity with actions. When I find their poses provocative, in a dramatic sense, I say, "Freeze."

As with the car mimic improvisation, I have 10-12 students lined up, ready to enter the stage. When I say, "Freeze," the students on stage freeze in their final positions. The next student enters and chooses which student he wants to tap out. He assumes this student's position, and here's where the improvisation becomes interesting. The new student, while in the same position as the previous student, must create a new scene, one that is different in tone and mood than the previous one. Perhaps the karate instruction scene becomes a robbery scene. It's important that the students let the poses dictate the new scene. They should not have premeditated ideas. It's also important to stress to students that they must do something in the scene. If they just stand and speak, there will be no reason to say, "Freeze." The more they do, the more opportunities there are for interesting freezes, which then lead to more unusual, less predictable scenes.

50. Freeze Tag, Adding Students

Sometimes it's interesting to add students, creating scenes with three, four and five students. In this improvisation, the two students on stage freeze, but the student who comes in doesn't tap anyone. He looks at the positions of the two people on stage, and based on what he sees, he starts a new scene, this time with three students. You can continue this until you have five people on stage. Keep in mind something, however. When you add students you run the risk of creating a scene that is too chaotic. It becomes challenging to the students to share the stage, to give and take accordingly. More often than not I see this improvisation fail because students want to talk at the same time. Nonetheless, it is worth trying this variation because it teaches the students how to share the stage.

51. Freeze Tag Reverse

If you have some advanced students you might try this one. It's essentially the previous improvisation, with an added twist. Students perform the two-person, three-person, four-person and five-person scenes, and then they continue in reverse. In other words, after the last student creates a new scene, he must find a reason to leave. As soon as he leaves, the students immediately go back to the four-person scene, and then when the fourth student leaves they return to the three-person scene. Finally, after the third person leaves there will be the original two students on stage, and they will resume their two-person scene. This one works very well when each of the scenes is distinctly different in tone and subject. It's fun to see the students make sharp and sudden changes from one scene to the next. Again, you might try this one with some of your more advanced students.

52. Emotion Arms

Have one student stand with his arms behind his back. A second student stands behind him and becomes the front student's arms. I like to do this one with four pairs on stage. Each student in the foreground is given an emotion. Each one must tell an exaggerated story. The people behind the speakers must use their arms in very specific gestures. Movements of the arms should not be general, such as just waving your arms. They must be specific:

153

rubbing the temples, taking off glasses, wiping brow. A have a tapper stand behind the speakers. He moves around, tapping one to speak, then tapping another to speak. In this format there will be four simultaneous, rotating stories. If the first speaker is telling a story about fear, the next one is telling a story about confidence or power. It's important to have contrasting emotions, so that the mood and tone of each of the stories varies. I also recommend for his improvisation to pair up two students who are physically very different. Have a very tall man paired with a short girl, meaning the man speaking, although big, has tiny arms, or vice versa.

53. Emotion Arms Mimic

For this one, I use three pairs of students. (I will refer to them as A, B, C.) Each pair is given an emotion. The speaker speaks; the person using the arms moves accordingly. In this format, after A finishes, B mimics A, using the same words and tone and the same arms and hands. The C pair then initiates a new story, and this time the A pair mimics C. Finally, the B pair performs its scene, and the C pair mimic them.

54. Emotion Mimic

I use three tables, one pair (A, B, C) at each table. Each pair is given an emotion and plays a short scene (20 seconds), expressing its emotion. After the A pair performs its scene, the B pair mimics them. Then after the C pair performs its scene, the A pair mimics them. Finally, the B pair performs its emotion scene, and the C pair mimics them.

55. Props Used Imaginatively

Numerous formats can be used for this improvisation. I favor using three tables on stage, two chairs at each. I place a dozen or so props on stage, the more random and varied the props, the better. Three pairs of students sit at the tables. I have an assistant hand the first pair a prop. The pair must use that prop imaginatively in ten seconds. I say, "Pass." The middle pair receives the same prop. They must now use the prop imaginatively, differently than the first pair.. Finally I say, "Pass," at which time the last pair receives the prop, using it differently than the preceding pairs. I rotate who receives the prop first. Sometimes the students start in the middle or the opposite end. This improvisation should be fast-moving. The students come up with a quick choice or idea. In ten seconds it's over, and we're moving on to the next prop.

56. Props Used Literally

For this one I have the students perform a two-person scene. I lay out five props. The students are instructed to use all five props in the scene. They shouldn't use them rapidly or mechanically. They must integrate them naturally, at the right time, as the moment in the scene dictates. In other words, the props should be extensions of what's happening in the scene in terms of the established relationship and its behaviors.

57. Using Costume Accessories

Two students perform multiple scenes in this improvisation. On stage, I place a clothing rack, which includes wigs and hats as well as dresses, shirts, jackets, etc. I instruct the students to wear an accessory, and as they do they create characters and begin a scene that will last no longer than 20 seconds. At that point, they change accessories and in doing so create another scene. In one minute they should be able to perform several scenes, allowing the costume accessories to influence their choices.

58. Give Me That Chair

This one includes a great many students and also involves audience participation. One student sits in a chair. I have 10-12 students line up and come in one at a time, trying to get the chair from the student who is sitting. How does each student try to get the chair? He must say something clever and imaginative, something truly deserving to get the chair. He can't just say, "Hey, I broke my leg, can I have that chair?" The audience will say "No" to that. What constitutes winning the chair? Well, there isn't a formulaic response. When you hear it you will know. I know that sounds vague, but sometimes it's hard to explain brilliance. You have to see it and hear it. I will say this: It should be difficult to win the chair. A student should have to make up a fascinating reason or story to get the chair. If a student does win the chair, he then sits down until someone else comes along and tries to win the chair.

59. Give Me that Prop

This one uses the same idea as the previous one, except here the student who enters is trying to get the prop that is being held by the person who is on stage sitting. If his reason to get the prop is outrageous and creative and imaginative he gets the prop and he also sits down. If the student on stage is holding a shovel, the student who enters must have a very good reason why he should be given the shovel. The class typically votes yes or no. Though the audience should be hard to persuade, it must be open to students whose reasons clearly are original and highly creative.

60. Same Character Storytelling

In this improvisation, all five students who are seated assume the same character. In other words, all five students are the same body builder, the same Italian chef, etc. They have the same mannerisms, the same texture of voice, etc. I use the tapper for this one as well. One student starts the story, perhaps a sentence or two; the tapper then passes the story to another student, and so on. This one challenges the students in ways that Judgment Day doesn't. It stretches students' physical and vocal ranges, while requiring mimic and observation skills. Just as importantly, it engages their imaginations, as they must continue a story spontaneously, having to add new twists as they do.

61. Switching Emotion Storytelling

While there are many types of emotion storytelling, the one I favor is as follows: five students seated in chairs are instructed to tell a continuous story. In other words, one student starts a story in an emotion given to him. The next student who is tapped continues the story in the same emotion. I will quickly change the emotion. And I'll keep changing the emotion while the story continues. The object here is two-fold: I want the story to be dramatically interesting and entertaining. Switching from terrified to enthusiastic to annoyed combats the improvisation growing stale. At the same time, I want my students to stretch their emotional ranges. To assure student flexibility and range, I'll call out contrasting emotions. I'm less concerned about the veracity of the story and more interested in the students' emotional investments, in their playfulness, in their using verbal and nonverbal communication

62. Word Tennis

This one is more of a word game and a competition than it is an improvisation. As the title suggests, competitors play a game of tennis with words. It works best with two teams, 10-12 students on each team. A student from each team stands center stage, side-by-side. I call out a category, perhaps "ice cream flavors". One at a time, alternating, each competitor names an ice cream flavor. The object of the competition is for one of them to outlast the other. The game needs to move quickly. The first one to stall or stop or repeat a word that's already been said loses. I give a point to the winning team. Then the next two students in their teams' lines step to the center of the stage. I call out another category, and the students begin playing this tennis match with words. I tend to use fairly simple categories, to assure the students can provide many words. If I call out European novels, the match may end before it begins.

Thus, I stick to what the students know. Here's a sampling of categories I typically use:

Ice cream flavors	Countries
Languages	Cereal brands
U.S. cities	Superheroes
Sports	Colleges
Shoe brands	Animals
Colors	Celebrities
Vegetables	Fast foods
Fruits	Song titles

63. Genre Storytelling

Five students sit in chairs facing the audience. I assign different (contrasting) genres to the students, telling them to communicate, in their assigned genres, a continuous story. I remind them they need to physicalize—not only verbalize —the story. As in previous storytelling formats, I once again utilize the services of a tapper who must be aware of the desired contrasting tones, from one student to the next. This one works especially well if I choose the right genres, and if the tapper switches in a timely fashion. Switching from Children's Story to Hip Hop to Shakespeare to Surfer to Opera can't help but add exciting, not to say entertaining, twists in the story. An alternative I've used is not to assign genres to each student. I have them tell a continuous story as I call out genres randomly, sometimes switching genres on the same student.

64. Genre Pairs

I place six pairs of students in various areas of the stage. Five of the pairs are given a genre. The pair without a genre begins the improvisation with a conversation. I usually suggesting something, such as "Why don't you want to be my friend?" The words they communicate will be the words used by all the pairs. The scene has to be short, no more than 30 seconds. Otherwise, the others will not be able to memorize the words. Once the initial scene is complete, I have the other pairs perform the same script, in their gen-res. If the genres are performed well—with a distinct tone, sound and appropriate gestures—each scene will be fresh and original, even though the words are the same. I have probably mentioned this before, but it's worth mentioning again. Anytime I use genres or emotions I make sure I give contrasting ones. Here's an order that will assure changes in style, voice and physical mannerisms:

Thriller →	Sea adventure →	Valley girl
Horror →	Children's story →	Action

65. Two-Person Mimics

Two students sit at a table stage right, and two at the table stage left. This one is a mimic improvisation. Therefore, students must watch and listen intently. The students who sit stage left perform a 30 second scene, with demonstrable emotions and actions. The students stage right then per-form the same scene, with the exact emotions and actions as their predecessors. After their mimic is complete, I then have the students who sit stage right perform a 30 second scene, while the students sitting stage left perform the mimic. Make sure the students know which specific stu-dent they're mimicking.

66. Group Story Gibberish Translation

Twelve students stand in a line, facing the audience. The object for the group is to tell a sensible, continuous story, alternating between gibberish and English translation. Here's the format: the odd numbered students speak gib-berish and the even-numbered students translate gibberish into English. The story itself, in English, is only 6 sentences. When the group finishes, I have the students switch positions. Those who were the translators are now telling a continuous story in gibberish. And those who were the gibberish speakers are now the translators of the new story.

67. Group Gibberish Song

This one is nearly the same as the previous one, with one exception: the students sing in gibberish, and the translators sing in English. Otherwise, the song, just as the preceding story, must make sense.

68. Three-Person Gibberish with Host

One of the students is the Host of the show. His guest comes from a land where only gibberish is spoken. Therefore, the guest must bring his translator. Here's how it works: The Host introduces the guest, giving the audience some background about where the guest is from. The guest's translator comes on, as well, and sits next to the guest. The Host asks the guest a question, in English, of course. Well, the guest does not understand English. Therefore, the translator must translate to the guest, speaking gibberish with him. After the guest responds to the translator, the translator then communicates to the Host, telling him what the guest said, in answer to his question. You will need clever students for this improvisation. The Host must know the best questions to ask, and the translator must speak both English and gibberish, knowing that his translations make or break the scene.

69. Gibberish Poem

This improvisation uses two students on stage, one speaking gibberish, the other translating. Here the gibberish person is reciting a poem. It's very important that he follows the three proper guidelines for gibberish: clear sound, specific gestures and definitive tone. He speaks his poem one sentence at a time. The translator translates. The poem can be about any subject. Sometimes the class will suggest a topic or title, such as "An Ode to a Shoe" or something unusual.

70. Voice Over

For this improvisation you will need students who are not only adept at pantomime, but equally skilled at hearing and reacting so quickly that it appears that they are the ones who are speaking, when, in reality, the voices are coming from others. Two students sit side-by-side, center stage. Two speakers also stand on stage, one far left (the voice of the person sitting left) and one far right (the voice of the person sitting right). The execution of this improvisation is challenging. The students sitting in the center are engaged in a conversation. They must move their mouths and bodies, taking their cues from the speakers. The speakers have a significant role, as well. They must provide clever storytelling and suitable expression for those who are pantomiming. They must shift emotional gears throughout to assure that the dialogue and action between the center stage students is vital and entertaining. It's critical in this improvisation that the students doing the pantomime keep their faces out to the audience. The audience must be able to see their faces and mouths clearly. If they turn to each other, as people in actual life might do, their communication will be lost.

71. Can't Say I, Me, My, Mine

This improvisation uses word limitations. Two students begin a scene and must continue sensibly without saying I, Me, My or Mine. This improvisation works well when I use it as a contest or competition. I place five pairs of students on stage. One at a time, each pair begins and develops a scene to see how long they can last without saying one of the words. Someone in the audience keeps time. I rotate the students on stage until everyone in the class has participated. Of course, this one doesn't have to be used as a competition, but it's just a personal preference I make with it.

72. Questions Only

Here's another popular limitation improvisation. Two students begin and develop a scene that must be told entirely in questions. The challenge here is that students must create a scene that makes sense. It shouldn't be repetitive, redundant or nonsensical. Again, as with the previous limitation improvisation, I use the same contest format, placing many pairs on stage and have them perform their scene one at a time, continuing until everyone has participated.

73. One Knows, One Doesn't

This is a who, what, where improvisation in which one of the participants knows the who, what, where and the other doesn't.

For the sake of simplicity, I'll refer to the one who knows as A and the one who doesn't as B. The improvisation begins with the B student leaving the room. While he is gone, I tell the A student who he is, where he is, and what his relationship to the other person is. This is a hard improvisation because the A student should never be overt about who he is in relation to B. When the B student comes on stage he enters with no predetermined ideas about the who, what, and where. He has to take his cues (the hints) from the A student. The A student must give hints but not make it obvious. For instance, here's a situation. The A student is a prison warden. The B student is a prisoner who is going to be executed that morning. The B student, when he enters, has no idea who he is, but when the A student begins speaking to him, he must at some point make a choice. He cannot remain neutral, and he is not allowed to ask questions. The A student must speak in generalities. In other words, he should purposely talk and ask questions that could be about anything. If he says, "Are you ready?" the B student cannot say, "For what?" He has to make a choice. A better choice would be "I'm ready if you're ready." The A student would then say, "Oh, don't worry, I've been ready for this day for a long time." The B student might respond, "That makes two of us." In his mind, the B student might think the scene is about two students graduating from high school, and this is exactly the type of scene you want. The A student knows, and the audience knows, and the B student thinks he knows, but really doesn't. If you can create that type of irony in the improvisation, it will be humorous and effective. To have this desired result, each player must effectively perform his part.

74. The Host and Audience Know but the Guest Doesn't

This one, though similar to the previous one, uses audience participation. The difference here is that this one is not a scene. It is designed and executed as an interview, such as one might see on a late-night talk show. The A student, this time, is the host. The B student leaves the room and while he does I reveal to the host and the class B' character. For example, I say that B is Satan. The host must ask questions and make comments that could suggest that B is anyone. B cannot be neutral. He must receive the questions and comments and make a specific choice about his character.

After the host and guest talk for a while, the host then opens the interview to the audience. Anyone in the class can ask questions to the guest, as long as these questions are not too obvious in revealing B's character. The host might say, "Welcome, I must say I like your tan." B says, "Thank you, I try to get as much sun as possible." A responds, "Is that right? I didn't think you got a lot of sun where you lived." The irony can lead to many humorous exchanges. The improvisation continues until B guesses his character. Of course, you don't want it to last forever.

At some point, if B can't guess, I'll instruct the Host and the audience to make it obvious through blatant questions.

75. Party Guessing Game

One student is hosting a party where there will be five guests. The host leaves the room and while he is gone, the guests receive, either from the audience or me, characters.

For instance, one might be a priest, one might be the host's parole officer, one might be his lawyer, etc. The object of the improvisation is for the host to guess each guest's character. The guests come on stage one a time and engage the host in conversation. Just as in the previous improvisations, the guests must give hints about who they are, but never reveal themselves too overtly. It shouldn't be too easy for the host to guess. On the other hand, each guest must give hints. Otherwise, they will make it impossible for the host. A fine balance must be struck. The host should spend no more than 30 seconds with each guest. If the hints are good and the host is clever he will guess the guest's character. The first guest sits down, and the next guest enters to converse with the Host. Guessing games are very entertaining as long as the players give clever hints, revealing something but not too much. For instance, if a guest is a priest he shouldn't come in and say, "I Think it's a good idea if we all pray before the party begins." It would be too obvious that he's a priest. An interesting beginning might be the following: The Host says, "Welcome, I am your host." The priest says, "Host? That's funny. Usually I am your host, if you know what I mean." This beginning might start a humorous exchange, and leave room for interpretations and guesses.

76. The Dating Game

Here's another popular guessing game. Three students of the same gender sit in adjoining chairs. One student of the opposite gender sits in a chair separate from the others, in a position where he or she cannot see the others. Before the improvisation begins, the contestant leaves the room. During this time, the three guests receive characters. The contestant returns and begins asking questions to each guest, all the time trying to guess their characters. Let's say, for instance, that the first guest is—once again—Satan. The contestant asks, "Guest number one, where would you like to go on a first date?" A good response would be "Some place hot." This response gives a hint about his character but it's also general enough to be interpreted many ways. I suggest doing the dating game twice, once each with male and female contestants.

77. Beginning Line

As the title suggests, this two-person improvisation begins with a line that is general enough to allow the scene to have multiple meanings and interpretations. I usually make this one a 45 second improvisation. The students have to make instant decisions about character, place and relationship. It has to begin and resolve itself in less than a minute. Here's a sampling of lines I might use:

1. So, what do we do now?
2. You're not going to like what I have to say.
3. I need to tell you something important.
4. Time is running out. We either do it or we don't.
5. You know what I'm thinking about right now?
6. It's time for you and me to have a talk.
7. So, what you're telling me is I'm not needed anymore.
8. I need you to listen to what I have to say.
9. Sit down and pay attention, a decision has to be made.
10. Don't call me that, I hate when you call me that.
11. The sun is about to set. What should we do?
12. I'm not going to stay here and listen to you vent.
13. We've been friends a long time, haven't we?
14. I'm sorry that you feel that way about me.
15. Are you sure? You might be imagining it?

78. Speed Alteration Scene

This improvisation repeats itself three times, each successive one becoming faster. The instructions are as follows: two students develop a scene that includes dialogue and actions, such as sitting, standing, and moving, etc. It doesn't really matter what the scene is about. What's important is that it's 45 seconds and includes dialogue and actions. After the students finish the 45-second scene, I have them repeat the same scene in 25 seconds. Of course, in order to do the same scene, dialogue and actions included, they must speed up, talk and move faster. After they finish the 25-second scene, they perform the same scene in 15 seconds. It's a humorous improvisation to watch as students adapt to the changing time restrictions. I don't always use a 45-25-15 format. I sometimes use 30-20-10.

79. Opposite Emotions

I prefer to do this improvisation with two students on stage, one left and one right. I give each student an emotion, making sure they receive opposite ones. For instance, one is happy and one is sad. Each student is telling his own story, according to his emotion, and they speak one sentence at a time, switching back and forth quickly. Here's a brief example, referring to the sad one as A and the happy one as B:

> A: *"I can't believe I lost again."*
> B: *"I always win!"*
> A: *"I'm such a loser."*
> B: *"Life is perfect for me right now."*
> A: *"I don't know why I even bother."*
> B: *"I can't wait to get out of bed and start my day."*

It's important in this improvisation that the students play off each other and exaggerate their emotions. Even though they are not engaged in conversation together, they must be aware of each other's energy and expression. It only works if the tones and words and actions are on opposite ends of the emotional spectrum. To mix things up a little, to make the exercise even more improvisational, I'll often say, "Switch," at which time the sad student suddenly becomes happy and the happy one suddenly becomes sad. I can switch as often or as little as possible, or not at all.

80. Same Situation, Different Emotions in Pairs

Similar to the previous improvisation, this one uses two pairs of students. I usually have them sit at tables on opposite sides of the stage. For this one I'll give them the same situation with accompanying opposite emotions. For instance, I tell each pair—a couple in this situation—that they are at a restaurant. One of the couples is having an argument and the other is enjoying a romantic evening. What makes this improvisation humorous is the switching back and forth. As we begin to hear and see the warmth and tenderness at one table, I'll switch the scene to the arguing couple. Sometimes I have them speak a few lines at a time, sometimes more. As in the previous improvisation, I'll also switch the couples' emotions. The arguing couple will become suddenly romantic and the romantic couple will argue instantly when I say "Switch." As well as being entertaining for the audience to watch and hear, it's a good exercise for the students involved, having to switch their tones and words and actions so instantly.

81. Two-Person Contrasting Motivations

I give students a situation where they have contrasting motivations. For example, they could be a couple planning a wedding, but in disagreement about where the service should take place. One wants to have a traditional wedding in a church. The other wants to have the wedding on a mountain, where the guests would have to hike to get there. This improvisation requires each student to support his argument with reasons, behaviors and actions. The improvisation should be no longer than two minutes. I often hold class contests with this one. I use a round robin single elimination format. Winners in the first round go against each other in the second round, and I continue with third, fourth and fifth rounds, until one student is crowned the class champ. Here are some sample ideas I use:

1. A couple disagrees about where to eat dinner. One wants to go out, and one wants to stay home and

make dinner.

2. Two friends find a sack of money. One wants to turn it in to the police. The other wants to keep the money and split it between them.

3. A couple wants to buy a pet. One wants to get a dog; the other wants a cat.

4. A couple just got married, but they can't agree where to live. One wants to live in the heart of the city, and the other wants the serenity of the countryside.

5. Two prisoners are in jail. One wants to break out. The other thinks it's better to stay.

6. One student acquires answers to a test. He thinks it's a good idea for him and his friend to cheat because it will result in their receiving higher grades. The other person refuses to cheat, under any condition.

7. Two school administrators discuss a student's punishment. One wants to expel the student. The other believes in giving the student another chance.

8. Two people witness a crime. One wants to report it. The other is afraid to report it.

9. Two seniors in high school disagree about where they should attend college. One wants to attend a school 3,000 miles away. The other thinks it's a better idea to stay close to home.

82. Two-Person Conflict Tag Team

This improvisation is essentially the same as the previous one, except it is done in a tag team format. I choose one of the conflicts that involve opposite genders and have the males and females line up on opposite sides of the stage. Two students begin this improvisation. Let's say it's the disagreement about where to get married, in a church or on a mountain. In the tag team format, any girl or boy in the line can come on stage and tag the initial student. The new student brings in fresh ideas and reasons to further his argument. A boy can then tag out the one who started the scene. Here it's not just one person with all the reasons and ideas. An entire team, one individual at a time, has the same motivation. Usually the two-person improvisation is over quickly, but in the tag team format it can—and should —last longer because there are many more contributors.

83. Language Translation

This is a good improvisation if you have a culturally mixed group and students who can speak in their native tongues. It is similar to gibberish translation, except students are not speaking gibberish. They are speaking a language that no one else in the class understands. For example, typically in my classroom I have students who speak fluent Tagalog, Arabic and Spanish. I will have two or three (perhaps more) students stage left performing a brief scene in one of these languages, and on the other side of the stage I place the same number of students who will translate the scene into English. Students must follow the same guidelines as they do in gibberish. They must use actions that are specific, and they must speak in clear, interpretive tones.

84. Playing Cards Status

I give to students, in pairs, random numbers from a deck of cards. I instruct each pair to perform a short improvisation, playing the status indicated by the card they receive. A 2 of any kind is the lowest status, and an Ace of any kind is the highest status. The class watches the improvisation and then guess which cards were given to the students.

Status is not always black and white. For example, it's not always determined by who has a higher position in society. It can be—and often is—determined by who has more emotional, physical and psychological leverage. Thus, a homeless person could conceivably have more status than a bank president if the homeless person is able to strike fear into the bank president and convince him to hand over money. Also, a teenager, through manipulative behavior, can easily have more status than a parent. I explain this because I don't want my students to play status in a cliché way. I want them to consider and use the full range of emotional, physical and psychological behaviors that allow one person to have more status than another. These are often fascinating improvisations because the students performing must interpret their cards and do a suitable scene, and the students watching get to analyze what they see and explain their interpretations, which are often very different than the performers'.

85. Guess the Speaker's Status

I use the deck of cards again. This time, I don't have students perform scenes. I have five students sit in chairs, facing the audience. I give each student a status card and tell them they will, one at a time, stand or sit and convey their status (character) to the audience, speaking and moving for 15-20 seconds. After each of the students performs, I then ask the class to guess the card each student received.

86. That's Not What Really Happened

Here's an improvisation that moves and changes in as many directions as you want. I start by giving two students a simple who, what and where situation. It might begin as follows: One student, a girl, is sitting down. The other student, a boy, walks in holding flowers. He says, "I bought you flowers because I love you very much." She cries and says, "Thank you, I love you, as well." They hug. At this point, I say, "Stop, that's not what really happened." I then proceed to tell them what really happened, and they have to perform it the way I describe it. For example, I say, "Yes, you did walk in a give her flowers, and you did say, 'I bought you flowers because I love you very much,' but her reaction was very different. Yes, she cried, but she did so because you should know better than to give her flowers. She's allergic to flowers. What really happened is she threw the flowers to the ground, slapped you and said she hated you."

After the students play the second scene as I described it, I will once again say, "Stop, that's not what really happened." I change the scene again. This improvisation can continue for a long time. I open up the directions to the entire class, meaning anyone in the class can say, "Stop" at any point and change what really happened.

87. The Movie Theater

For this one I will need students with the same kind of skills that were used in the Jake and Jim improvisation. Four students sit in chairs facing the audience. These students must be skilled at pantomime and nonverbal expression. They do not speak. They watch various movie genres, as if they were at a theater, and react to each one in exaggerated, dramatic ways. An advanced student stands to the side. He is the movie voice. His tone is everything in this improvisation since he is only heard, not seen. He must speak in ways that force the participants to react phrase by phrase, with their eyes, faces and bodies.

I call out a genre, starting with "Horror." The narrator begins, in an appropriate horror tone. "A young man is sitting on his couch. His parents are out for the evening. Suddenly the wind blows the front door open, the fireplace lights by itself, and the face of his first grade teacher appears, hanging from the ceiling like an oversized light bulb." The students sitting react with their best pantomime. After 15 seconds, I switch the movie, to another contrasting genre. I call out "Love Story." The narrator speaks: "Am I really the only love of your life? Yes, Carol. I've always loved you. Even when I didn't know you, I loved you. They kiss passionately, deeply; violins play, the sun comes out." In these two examples, the watchers' body language—facial expressions—should be measurably different, though equally engaging to the audience. I continue to change the movie every 15 seconds, though this time frame is flexible. If a moment on stage has magic in it, I allow it to play itself out. I take my cues from my performers. They often dictate how long or how short an improvisation should last.

88. Mr. Know it All

This one is a variation of the pattern improvisation. The biggest change is that here the five students are indeed one mind, and in this one they are not telling a story. They are answering a question from an audience member. The question must be one that elicits an inventive response from the students. For example, someone might ask, "Why is purple considered a spiritual color?" The students answer the question in whatever pattern I give them. Often I will have them answer the first question one word at a time. For the next question I might have them answer two words at a time. As I wrote for the previous improvisation, there are dozens, if not hundreds, of patterns I can give.

89. One Scene Ends in Tragedy

For this improvisation I use three tables, two chairs at each. Three pairs of students receive situations unknown to the audience. I tell the class one of the scenes will end tragically. The key to this improvisation is that each of the pairs must communicate a scene that has the look and sound of a situation that could end tragically. I huddle with the three pairs and give them situations and relationships, then choose the one that will end tragically.

When the students sit down at their tables, I tell the class who they are and how they're related. Let me give an example: the first pair is a couple that has been dating for close to a year. They are engaged. The second pair has been business partners for seven years. The last pair is a mother and son. I ask the class before we begin to guess which one will end tragically, based solely on the relationships. The pairs perform their scenes, one at a time, in installments. They must gradually build the tension in their scenes because they will have five turns, each one approximately 20 seconds, before the improvisation ends. Sometime in the middle of the improvisation, I will ask the class if anyone has changed their mind now that they've heard and seen some of the relationships. Not surprisingly, students do change their guess and even offer reasons why. This one is dependent on the students on stage. They must develop situations that are subtle and yet potentially dangerous.

90. Character Switches

Students switch roles whenever I say "Switch." The scene and story stays the same. One student might be a police interrogator and the other a suspect. When I say, "Switch" the police interrogator becomes the suspect right in the middle of a line, and the suspect becomes the police interrogator. I switch the characters many times or a few times, depending on how the scene is being played. Any number of situations can be used, such as the following:

1. Father/Son conflict
2. Basketball coach berating a player
3. Mother/Daughter talk
4. Therapist and a patient
5. Waiter and an irate customer
6. Priest in a confessional with a guilty parishioner
7. Nurse and a sick patient
8. Prisoner and a guard
9. Principal and a student
10. Director and an actor

91. Situation Switches

In the previous improvisation, two students play one situation, switching characters back and forth. In this improvisation, two students change situations and stories many times. I may have two students play a scene where they are old people in a nursing home. After 20 seconds, I switch the situation, saying, "You are now two small children opening presents on Christmas." At this point, I can further switch the situation, and, thus, their characters, or, if I want, I can switch back to the initial situation.

I'll allow the students to establish at least four different situations before I begin moving them back to previous ones. Here's an example of how I can create four situations for the same two students and then switch them around:

1. <u>First situation:</u> old people in a nursing home
2. <u>Second situation:</u> children opening presents on Christmas morning
3. <u>Third situation:</u> cooks in a busy, understaffed restaurant
4. <u>Fourth situation:</u> monks chanting prayer
5. <u>Second situation:</u> children opening presents on Christmas morning
6. <u>First situation:</u> old people in a nursing home
7. <u>Third situation:</u> cooks in a busy, understaffed restaurant

92. Sound Effects

Here is an improvisation I've done many different ways. Sometimes I have one student sit in the middle of a circle, the class around him. Someone begins with a sound effect. The student in the middle allows the sound effect to influence his choice: where he is, who he is, what is going on. The student may or may not speak, but he reacts to the changing sounds. At some point another student enters the circle. He communicates with the first student, both of them influenced by the sound effects they hear. I also do this improvisation with students sitting in the audience. I'll place two students to the side. These students make sound effects. Two other students are the players, responding to the sound effects. I favor the circle because anyone in the circle can enter the ring and join the lead student. The rule is that the improvisation centers on this one student. Other students enter briefly and interact with the lead student, but they quickly leave. I like the sound effect improvisation to look and sound like a dream. One person awakens to a sound or a series of changing sounds. He encounters various people or animals, whatever might be suitable for the sounds that are being created. This improvisation works well in an open time frame, depending on the creativity of the choices made by the players involved.

93. Simultaneous Experts

I use this improvisation as a competition. Two students stand adjacent to one another. I tell each student he is an expert on a particular subject. It doesn't matter what the subject is, as long as it's an appropriate one. What's important is that each student chooses something he can talk about freely and continuously because in this competition each student is speaking at the same time. The student who outlasts the other is the winner. It's important that students don't confuse talking with shouting. It's not the loudest speaker who wins. It's the student who talks nonstop. I tell the students to relax and let the words flow freely.

94. Animal Characterizations

This is a good improvisation for students looking to stretch their physical range. I give the students a simple situation. The focus here, however, is that they must integrate an animal into their character. I tell the students they remain human at all times. They still talk and walk like a human. What they're doing, however, is integrating an animal into their movements, into their speech. I tell them they are 60% human and 40% animal. If someone is a chicken in the scene, they do not become the chicken. Instead they are human with chicken characteristics. It doesn't matter what the scene is about. It could be two people meeting to rehearse a dance routine. One might be part snake, or part chicken, or part chimpanzee, or part penguin. As I said, this improvisation is especially a good one to get students to stretch their physical range, to discover movements, actions and voice textures they may not have been aware they possessed.

95. Limited to a Single Phrase

One of the players is limited to speaking just one line. He can say the line more than once, but it is the only line he can say. The challenge here is when he says it. Timing is everything if this one has a chance of being successful. If he says the line all the time it will lose its effect and the improvisation will not be funny. If he chooses the opportune time to say it, it can work very well. The other player can talk as much as he wants. He has to be aware that he is setting up the other student's response, and the student who is limited to one line has to know he is being set up. The line that the student speaks should be simple, such as "I would like that" or "I agree with you." This simple line works well with anything outrageous the other player says. In other words, you want a contrast, an irony, between what the players say. The students have to work together here. One is setting the other up. The other has to take the bait.

96. History Switches

This improvisation is similar in many ways to Environmental Switches. The focus here, however, is on historical moments. I place four students on stage and include chairs and tables if they need them. I begin by calling out a historical situation. I count to 8. The students decide their characters and arrange themselves. They improvise for 15 seconds. I call out another historical situation, repeating the process, counting to 8, allowing them this time to decide their characters and arrange themselves accordingly. This improvisation forces the students to work as a team. Each one of them cannot always be the leader. They must be a balanced team, continuously giving and taking. Here are some historical situations I give:

1. The Golden Age of Greece
2. The Roaring 20s
3. Pioneers
4. CavemenThe Civil War
5. The Renaissance
6. Ellis Island
7. Space travel
8. The Founding Fathers
9. The Industrial Revolution

97. Telephone Narration

The improvisation begins with a student telephoning someone and telling him about his extraordinary day yesterday. As he's talking about his day, a group of students act out what he says. For instance, if he says, "Well, the day started like any other day. I walked to the bus stop and sat down." As he narrates, a student sits down at the bus stop. The challenge for the students is striking a balance between the narrator and the actors. It shouldn't be a scene where the narrator is doing all the talking and the players are merely acting it out nonverbally. Sometimes the narrator speaks and sometimes the players speak. The narrator has to set up the actors to speak. If the narrator says, "I was sitting there humming a song to myself," the actor sitting down has to know that this is his cue to hum a song. If the narrator says "A man came and sat next to me. He said something strange to me," the actor coming into the scene has to know that this is his cue to speak and say something strange. This improvisation builds teamwork.

The narrator has the responsibility of setting up a good story, but the actors on stage must cleverly fill in the blanks by making creative verbal and nonverbal choices.

98. Revolving Scene, Adding Characters

I place two chairs on stage. These chairs are always occupied, but the actors are constantly revolving. As one student leaves, another student enters. The scene begins with two characters, such as a therapist and a patient. They have a quick interaction. The patient leaves. Another student enters. The therapist is still the same person. The new actor must create a character belonging to the therapist. For instance, he may be the therapist's husband. After a brief scene, the therapist leaves. The newest actor decides he's the husband's boss. As you can see, the students waiting in the wings must find a way to create a character who relates to and knows the previous character. It's a revolving scene, a continuous scene, always adding characters.

99. Evolving Emotions

This one is a 60 second improvisation that moves through emotional changes rather quickly. I give two students four emotions. Their scene must follow the order of these four emotions. For example, I tell two students that their scene has the following order: 1) it begins with a tone of frustration; 2) it becomes briefly happy; 3) the mood changes to suspicious; 4) the scene ends on a note of amazement. The challenge for the students is to perform the scene naturally, not formulaically.

100. Secrets

Each student is given a secret that he cannot reveal to the other person, but the secret is there and causes an internal conflict. Here's an example: I tell two students they're performing a scene between a husband and wife at a kitchen table. Privately, I tell each one something the other doesn't know. I tell the husband that he does not plan to go to work this day like he normally does. He has decided without telling his wife that he is going to stay home and just relax in the yard. He is hoping she will go out and do errands and won't notice that he doesn't go to work. This is his secret. Her secret is as follows: she desperately can't wait for him to go to work this morning because she is expecting a visitor. I don't specify the nature of the visitor.

I leave the choice to her. Most likely she'll interpret it to mean she is seeing a man, cheating on her husband. In any case, she wants him to leave and yet we know he has no intention of leaving. I want the audience to know both secrets, so after I tell the two actors their secrets I have them leave the room so I can tell the audience the situation. It's a very interesting improvisation because the students have hidden conflicts and motivations and these internal situations create wonderful subtext in their dialogue.

(Exercises continued on following page)

101. Telephone Rumors

This improvisation is performed entirely on telephones. I place 5 or 6 students in various stage areas. Their areas suggest different locations. One student starts by calling another student. Before long the information conveyed from one to another is changed as the scene progresses. The telephone callers need to keep the improvisation moving forward. To do this they must instigate each other and constantly invent new rumors and situations that cause problems. The scene should begin with the smallest of seeds—someone says something to someone else—which then grows into a forest of rumors.

102. Audience Determines What Happens Next

This improvisation can be called "Fill in the Blank." Two students on stage are given a situation. They begin a scene. At some point, someone in the audience says, "Stop." The audience person tells the actors what happens next. Here's an example of how it might play out: I give two students a situation. All I say is it's a scene about someone telling someone else they are under arrest. So the scene begins with a man sitting in his house. A woman comes in holding an imaginary gun, saying, "Don't move, you're under arrest." Suddenly, someone in the audience says, "Stop." He explains what happens next. He tells them this: "The man laughs and says to the woman, 'Edna, come off it, how many times do we have to play this game. You're not a detective and I'm not a suspect. I'm your husband and you're my wife. Can we please just have a relaxing evening for a change?' The students on stage play the scene as described to them, until someone else in the audience says "Stop" and adds the next chapter of the improvisation.

SECTION IV:
Small Group Improvisational Scenes and Activities

SECTION IV: FOREWARD

These scenes are designed for small groups and should be introduced and completed in one or two class periods. They are performed as improvisations. I do not include them in the Improvisation Section because they are small group exercises, and I allow the students several minutes or more to discuss their plan before they proceed. The scenes themselves are just a few minutes in length. Therefore, it is manageable to give these assignments and have them completed in a limited time frame.

SCENE-BASED ACTIVITIES

1. Therapist Flashback Scene

I place a table and two chairs stage left. The therapist sits behind the table, and the patient sits in the adjacent chair. The scene begins with the therapist asking the patient to review the critical moments in his life, those that seem to have shaped him the most, good or bad. Both the patient and the therapist are responsible for creating this improvisation, for opening the doors for people in the patient's life to appear, and to keep the scene moving along quickly, always introducing new characters and situations. The other three students in the scene must be flexible enough to play various roles, depending on where the therapist and patient take the scene. Here's what's needed for this scene:

Stage Left: Therapist, patient
Stage right: Three others who play various parts in the patient's flashbacks
The patient moves from stage left to stage right accordingly
The Suggested Order:
First Scene: patient, therapist
Second Scene: flashback
Third Scene: patient, therapist
Fourth Scene: flashback
Fifth Scene: patient, flashback
Sixth Scene: flashback
Seventh Scene: patient, therapist

2. Film Reviews Using Genres

The film reviewer sits center stage. He has the most important role, for he controls the flow of the scene. He must be astute and able to provide insightful commentary. He must develop his thoughts and have something meaningful to say in his introduction, before and after each film clip, and in his conclusion. Everyone else appears in the film clips that are approximately 20-30 seconds in length. These clips are shown stage left and right. The group must first decide on which five genres will be reviewed. For this assignment, I recommend that students rotate in film clips. It's desirable to have two students per film clip. Here's a list of genres I provide for the students:

Tragic love	Fantasy	Adventure
Urban	Spoof	Science Fiction
Horror	Romance	Children's story
Western	Animation	Heroes and heroines
Urban hip	Karate film	Natural disaster
Historical	Existential	Detective spoof
Musical	Teen movie	Classical language
Middle Ages	Mystery	Language translation

3. This is Your Life (6 students)

I borrow from the old TV show in creating this assignment. Two main people sit center stage: the host of the show and the main guest. The host of the show is the facilitator. He asks appropriate questions and keeps the scene moving forward. The main guest is the person whose life is highlighted. This person will interact with the host and all the participants who appear, surprisingly, from her life. The other 4 people are the participants who come on one at a time. Each is significant—in a good or bad way—in the main guest's life. It's recommended that the participants are four varied people from different times and ages in the main guest's life. It's equally important that these people are not predictable or ordinary in any way, such as the main guest's brother, sister or old elementary school teacher. Here are a couple of examples that are fresh and original:

- *"Do you remember that night in Las Vegas? No, of course you don't. You were too inebriated to remember that night. Well, we have someone here tonight who does remember what you did. The taxi cab driver that drove you to your hotel."*

- *"Do you remember being nine months old, falling out of a two-story building? How could you remember that? Well, the good Samaritan who caught you in his arms before you hit the ground is with us here tonight."*

These examples reflect the importance of avoiding the usual response and, in doing so, add a freshness and originality to the choices and improvisation.

4. News Show

This one may seem similar to the two-minute drill improvisation in the previous section. What's different, however, is that it's not a rapid-fire timed activity. This one is longer and more developed. The newscaster sits center stage. He is the most important person, for he controls the scene, presenting breaking news stories and providing appropriate commentary and analysis of events taking place in his local community and around the world.

The rest of group appears left and right, playing multiple roles: reporters, those being interviewed, etc. The news stories should be varied and uniquely imaginative, avoiding anything cliché or stereotypical.

5. Fortune Cookie Scene

One person appears on stage. He has just returned from a Chinese restaurant. He just now opens his fortune and reads it aloud. He leaves the stage without thinking the fortune could come true. The scene then proceeds with each group member playing one or more roles in the story, inventing a way to make the fortune come true. Here is a list of possible fortunes that can be used.

- One or more gods will pay you an unexpected visit. They will send you on an important mission to save the world.
- The ghost of your former spouse will suddenly ap-

pear to you. She will force you to reconsider your current re-marriage plans.

- You will travel to a foreign land where you will become emperor.
- You will find an object that will give you x-ray vision.
- You will change your voice and wear a hat. This change in your appearance will make you popular with the opposite sex.
- You will watch a TV ad that will change your life.
- You will receive a telephone call from an old friend. You will become suddenly wealthy.
- You will enroll in a new class. What you learn will help you discover your true potential.
- You will meet an old person who will ask you to solve an ancient riddle.
- You will begin to rhyme every sentence you speak. Furthermore, those who meet you will also rhyme their sentences.

6. Titles

Here is one I use numerous times throughout the year. I give each group a slip of paper with a title written on it. This title defines and shapes the scene. It's recommended, as well, that the line be used at the end of the scene. The following are titles I use:

1. What Really Happened to Jack and Jill?
2. Pride Goes Before a Fall
3. I Was a Teenage Girl Monster
4. There's a New Sheriff in Town
5. Why the Old Lady was Forced to Live in a Shoe
6. She does not Suffer Fools Gladly
7. Living in the Shadow of Paradise
8. The Bell Tolls for Thee, My Friend
9. Oh, Sisters of Mercy, Save my Blackened Soul
10. The Strange Case of Doctor No Good.
11. The Winds of Change Do Blow Through Me

12. Blessed Be that Rarest Flower, Forgiveness
13. I Never Promised You a Rose Garden
14. Butterflies Are Free. If only the Same were True for Me
15. Be Careful What You Wish For
16. Horror at the Wax Museum
17. The Last Opportunity
18. The Climb to the Top Is Easy. It's the Fall that's Hard
19. The Strange Case of the Missing iPhone
20. The Truth Before My Eyes

7. Situational Titles

This one is a slight variation from the previous assignment. Here I give each group a more specific situation. Here are some examples:

1. Right before the priest gives the wedding vows, the groom has second thoughts.
2. Someone wakes up on a park bench with amnesia.
3. A scientist returns to the past and changes a historical event.
4. A funeral service becomes macabre when people realize the body isn't dead.
5. A couple moves into a house occupied by ghosts.
6. A scene of mistaken identity causes mayhem at a restaurant.
7. Someone returns from war to discover his wife is remarried.
8. Someone returns home paralyzed after a car crash.
9. A physic performs a successful séance to a group of nonbelievers.
10. An alien from outer space visits a retired couple on a farm.

8. Emotion Statue

I assign each group of five students an emotion. Their task is to create a statue, one person at a time, and then tell a story one person at a time, suitable to the given emotion. The exercise will follow this format: The first student walks to center stage and strikes a pose. The next student comes out and adds to the picture. His pose is different than the first one, but it also contributes to the statue. The third person, and then the fourth and fifth, add until the statue is complete. The poses should be a composite of the given emotion. It should be a statue with five parts, not five random poses. Collectively the poses should tell a story. After the students come out one at a time and strike their poses, they begin their story. Each student speaks one sentence. He unfreezes, moves and speaks. Then freezes again. Next the second speaker unfreezes, moves and speaks. The group continues until everyone has spoken. At the end of the story, I tell them to freeze in their positions. The class then guesses the emotion.

9. Same Story in Different Genres (6 students)

This one is a follow up to the Emotion Statue assignment. The difference here is that the students will make a statue based on the genre I give, and for this one they will have a script they will speak. The focus here is on how they deliver the words. By this point students will have had sufficient practice with genres. Students will make a statue and tell the following story one speaker/voice at a time, in the tone and sound appropriate for the genre given. What's appealing here is that though each group has the same story and same words, their scripts should be uniquely different because each will have a distinct look and sound. Here's one of the simple stories I give:

1. The ocean waves, white like foam, broke high above the child.
2. His name was Billy. Billy Barton.
3. He was only three days old.
4. A giant wave cascaded high above his head and knocked him down.
5. He struggled to his feet and called his mother.

6. He called again and again, but she was nowhere in sight.

I always make sure to assign groups contrasting genres, such as children's story and horror, etc. to assure the scenes will stand out in relation to one another. If done well, the rest of the class should have an easy time guessing the genre.

10. Slide Show

I tell the students that as a group they traveled the world and took many pictures. In this assignment, they must show five unusual pictures, from very different places, to the class. This assignment requires a narrator to comment on each of the pictures and explain the circumstances of it. The group is frozen in its picture while the narrator is speaking. I recommend to each group that they rotate the narrator, thereby assuring that each person speaks. It's important here that the narrator doesn't merely explain what is literal to our eye. A story, albeit 20 seconds, must be told about each picture.

11. Moogie Mock

I introduce this assignment by asking the students to explain to me the meaning of a moogie mock. They usually come up with creative responses, until I tell them that a moogie mock is a brand of hair gel. The students look at me surprisingly. The truth is, I tell them, that a moogie mock could be anything they want it to be, since there is no such thing as a moogie mock. And that's the nature of this assignment. I give each group a slip of paper and ask them to create/invent a word that's easy to pronounce and to write it down. Once each group has written their invented word, I pass the words around to the various groups, making sure that each group does not wind up with the word it created. I give each group a few minutes to decide what type of product the word suggests. They must then create a two-minute commercial, with a clear beginning, middle and end. At the end of the commercial the group sings its jingle. Here's the order I suggest:

1. The first brief scene (30 seconds) should present the problem.
2. The second brief scene (30 seconds) should include the presence of the product, intended to fix the problem.
3. The third brief scene (30 seconds) shows the actual application of the product, and thus the resolution of the problem.
4. The fourth scene (30 seconds) drives the point home with its jingle.

12. Story Using Random Words (3 students)

I give each group a slip of paper with three randomly selected words written on it. With little preparation, the group must create a clever, cohesive story, 2-3 minutes, in which the three words are integrated so naturally that the rest of the class would never know they were selected randomly, with little relationship to each other. Here's an example of how it might develop: a group receives the words clock, bird and rope. The scene starts with two students carrying the third student. This student, it turns out, is a large cuckoo clock that the other two students purchased at a garage sale. The two students quickly learn that the clock is broken. When they move the hands of the clock to indicate each hour, a bird is supposed to come out of the clock's mouth. But the bird is apparently stuck inside the mouth of the clock. One of the students takes off the rope that he uses as a belt around his waist. He ties it to the bird that is stuck inside the clock's mouth. He gently pulls the rope until the bird appears. It turns out the bird was just stuck all along. The students move the hands of the clock to each hour, and now the bird appears and makes a cuckoo sound. The student puts his rope back on his pants. In this scenario, the students will have effectively integrated the three random words in a natural way without calling attention to the fact that they are unrelated.

Below are some groupings of words that I created and use. It will take only minutes to make dozens of these and write them on small slips of paper.

Clock	Pillow	Bowl
Bird	Lion	Hockey
Shoelace	Chair	Jelly
Rope	Castle	Rabbit
Radio	Box	Moon
Kite	Robot	Amplifier
Bookshelf	Rug	Telephone
Sailboat	Money	Screwdriver
Mailbox	Cat	Hammer
Napkin	Lettuce	Money
Carrot	Book	Butterfly
Monkey	Princess	Mice

13. Imaginative Use of Props

While I primarily include this one in the Improvisation section, I use it as well for group work. I give each group, ranging from 3-5 students, several props. By props, I mean anything I can pull out of one of my storage rooms: a broom, a dustpan, a towel, a lamp, a bottle, a vase, an iron, a hat, etc. It doesn't matter the size and shape of the prop. Any object is a prop for this assignment. The key component of this assignment is that the students must find a way to use this prop imaginatively. If it's a stick, they cannot use it as a stick. Perhaps the stick is a dinosaur bone that one of them found and is now trying to sell on Craigslist. While you can just as easily pass out props and have the students use the props literally and integrate them cleverly, as they do in the Three Words assignment, it is more fun to watch them come up with imaginative uses of props.

14. Wax Museum Figures

I present this assignment as a guessing game. I tell students in each group to draw from history and create a statue that might be universally recognizable. After the students talk it over for a few minutes, I have them all appear on stage at the same time, and then on my signal they freeze and become the wax museum figures, spreading out in various parts of the stage. I then select several students from other groups to be the visitors. One of these students is the museum's curator. He walks around with the visitors and explains (guesses) each historical character. After the curator and visitors leave, each statue comes to life and speaks briefly. By this time, if the curator hadn't guessed correctly, the wax figure's identity should become clear.

15. Time Machine

One student, the protagonist of the improvisation, steps into a time machine. He goes back to a specific moment in the past. Since he has lived in the future and knows well the outcomes and consequences of historical events—especially the one he encounters—he has an opportunity to change the outcome and, thus, alter history. For instance, maybe he arrives in the theater before John Wilkes Booth assassinates Abraham Lincoln. He can prevent the tragedy from occurring, even though people then will probably think him mad for insinuating that such a tragedy will occur unless someone stops it. In any case, this group improvisation centers on the travails of this character. The others in the group will play the historical characters. I recommend using five students total. The scene should end with the protagonist returning to the present and listening to a news broadcast which proves that history has been changed. Here are some ideas that have worked well in my classroom:

1. Go back in time to prevent Adam and Eve from eating the apple.
2. Go back to prevent the White Man from taking Indian lands.
3. Go back to prevent the Romeo and Juliet tragedy.
4. Go back to prevent the sinking of the Titanic.

5. Go back to prevent Lincoln from getting shot in the theater.
6. Go back to bring antibiotics to prevent the death of a poor Victorian child with tuberculosis.

16. Meet Your Neighbors

This scene is designed for four students, two couples. One of the couples has lived in their house for a long time. They notice that new neighbors have moved in next door. The scene centers on the day the new neighbors come over to meet the couple that lives next to them. These couples should be as opposite as any two couples can be. Their values, attitudes, personalities and interests are on other ends of the compatibility spectrum. The traits they possess should be exaggerated as much as possible.

17. The Reunion, Using Dramatic Irony

Five people meet at a reunion. On the surface everyone is friendly towards one another, saying what's polite. During the scene, each player, at some point, will step down while the others freeze on stage. This person will reveal what he is really thinking. This is the classic Shakespearean aside moment, which is why it's called dramatic irony, since we the audience know what the characters are really thinking and planning, as opposed to what they say to the others. While I call this one a reunion, it can just as easily be a party, a school detention, a rehearsal or any place where five people might gather.

18. House Improvisation Scene

While this one is included in the improvisation section, it can also be performed as a small group assignment. Therefore, I'm going to repeat much of the same informa-tion as I did in Part 2 because, depending on my students, it may be more suitable to have them perform the scene in groups. Here then are the directions, somewhat modified for group participation: One student (the main person) is on stage the entire scene. The scene begins with this person walking on stage and showing her state of mind, through actions and behaviorisms, given the situation or problem she is given.

Here's a situation I might give: "You enter your house after walking home, believing that someone is following you." Next come telephone calls, one at a time, from the rest of the group. These calls should further instigate or complicate the main person's problem. Telephone calls should be made throughout the scene. As well as making calls, each person in the group should, at some point, enter the scene with the main person. He should make his visit brief, however. No more than two students, including the main person, should be on stage at one time. It's important that this scene moves quickly from telephone calls to visits. No call or visit should last more than 20-30 seconds.

Here are some suggestions for problems or situations:

- Someone is following you.
- You witnessed a crime.
- It's your birthday yet no one acknowledged it.
- You found a suitcase full of money.
- You just got fired from your job.
- You were driving home from work; you ran over your neighbor's dog.
- You just came back from the doctor; you received bad news.
- You received a bad haircut.
- Your car broke down; you are forced to stay at a strange motel.
- You just got home from school; no one asked you to the prom.
- You are a thief; someone allows you to use this place as a hideout.

19. Emotion Storytelling

The following stories have eight sentences. Each one should look and sound differently, according to the emotion highlighted. Five of the sentences should be spoken solo, by individual students. The other three sentences should be spoken in unison by the group.

The students decide which three are in unison and which five are solo. All sentences should be spoken clearly and audibly. The emotions should stand out, exaggeratedly. Each group should stage in a way that reflects the story and emotions. I provide seven different emotional patterns. Each group of 5 students is given a different pattern.

Story #1 (Version 1)

1. **Angry:** The boy—his name was Roger—ran as fast as he could.
2. **Happy:** The rain fell in swirls, hard on his head.
3. **Suspicious)** But he did not stop to seek shelter. He couldn't.
4. **Amazed:** The monster pursued him fast and furiously.
5. **Determined:** He cleared the forest and came to the edge of a cliff.
6. **Silly**: He knew he had no choice. He had to jump.
7. **Shocked:** And as he did, his eyes opened wide, in his bed.
8. **Courageous:** "Thank god," he said. "It was just a dream, just a dream."

Story #1 (Version 2)

1. **Paranoid**: The boy—his name was Roger—ran as fast as he could.
2. **Enthusiastic**: The rain fell in swirls, hard on his head.
3. **Frustrated**: But he did not stop to seek shelter. He couldn't.
4. **Loving**: The monster pursued him, fast and furiously.
5. **Angry**: He cleared the forest and came to the edge of a cliff.
6. **Amazed**: He knew he had no choice. He had to jump.

7. **Powerful**: And as he did, his eyes opened wide, in his bed.
8. **Excited**: "Thank god," he said. "It was just a dream, just a dream."

Story #1 (Version 3)
1. **Happy**: The boy—his name was Roger—ran as fast as he could.
2. **Terrified**: The rain fell in swirls, hard on his head.
3. **Irritated**: But he did not stop to seek shelter. He couldn't.
4. **Shocked**: The monster pursued him fast and furiously.
5. **Ambitious**: He cleared the forest and came to the edge of a cliff.
6. **Hateful**: He knew he had no choice. He had to jump.
7. **Silly**: And as he did, his eyes opened wide, in his bed.
8. **Paranoid**: "Thank god," he said. "It was just a dream, just a dream."

Story #1 (Version 4)
1. **Powerful**: The boy—his name was Roger—ran as fast as he could.
2. **Pleading**: The rain fell in swirls, hard on his head.
3. **Cheerful**: But he did not stop to seek shelter. He couldn't.
4. **Disbelieving**: The monster pursued him fast and furiously.
5. **Tense**: He cleared the forest and came to the edge of a cliff.
6. **Amazed**: He knew he had no choice. He had to jump.
7. **Disgusted**: And as he did, his eyes opened wide, in his bed.
8. **Happy**: "Thank god," he said. "It was just a dream, just a dream."

Story #1 (Version 5)
1. **Happy**: The boy—his name was Roger—ran as fast as he could.
2. **Stupid**: The rain fell in swirls, hard on his head.
3. **Energetic**: But he did not stop to seek shelter. He couldn't.
4. **Nervous**: The monster pursued him fast and furiously.
5. **Powerful**: He cleared the forest and came to the edge of a cliff.
6. **Shocked**: He knew he had no choice. He had to jump.
7. **Silly**: And as he did, his eyes opened wide, in his bed.
8. **Angry**: "Thank god," he said. "It was just a dream, just a dream."

Story #1 (Version 6)
1. **Shocked**: The boy—his name was Roger—ran as fast as he could.
2. **Determined**: The rain fell in swirls, hard on his head.
3. **Paranoid**: But he did not stop to seek shelter. He couldn't.
4. **Excited**: The monster pursued him fast and furiously.
5. **Hateful**: He cleared the forest and came to the edge of a cliff.
6. **Pleading**: He knew he had no choice. He had to jump.
7. **Frustrated**: And as he did, his eyes opened wide, in his bed.
8. **Terrified**: "Thank god," he said. "It was just a dream, just a dream."

Story #2 (Version 1)

1. **Angry**: I stood high on the hill, looking below at the crashing waves.

2. **Happy**: Lucy walked up to me, grinning from ear to ear.
3. **Suspicious**: "I've been stung by a bumble bee," she said.
4. **Amazed**: She began to flail her arms and buzz like the bee that had stung her.
5. **Determined**: "Lucy," I called to her, "stop acting crazy."
6. Silly: She didn't hear me; she didn't want to hear me.
7. **Shocked**: She flew off the hill, towards the crashing waves.
8. **Courageous**: And as she did, all I saw was a giant bee disappearing in the mist of the ocean water.

Story #2 (Version 2)

1. **Paranoid**: I stood high on the hill, looking below at the crashing waves.
2. **Enthusiastic**: Lucy walked up to me, grinning from ear to ear.
3. **Frustrated**: "I've been stung by a bumble bee," she said.
4. **Loving**: She began to flail her arms and buzz like the bee that had stung her.
5. **Angry**: "Lucy," I called to her, "stop acting crazy."
6. **Amazed**: She didn't hear me; she didn't want to hear me.
7. **Powerful**: She flew off the hill, towards the crashing waves.
8. **Excited**: And as she did, all I saw was a giant bee disappearing in the mist of the ocean water.

Story #2 (Version 3)
1. **Happy**: I stood high on the hill, looking below at the crashing waves.
2. **Terrified**: Lucy walked up to me, grinning from ear to ear.
3. **Irritated**: "I've been stung by a bumble bee," she said.

4. **Shocked**: She began to flail her arms and buzz like the bee that had stung her.
5. **Ambitious**: "Lucy," I called to her, "stop acting crazy."
6. **Hateful**: She didn't hear me; she didn't want to hear me.
7. **Silly**: She flew off the hill, towards the crashing waves.
8. **Paranoid**: And as she did, all I saw was a giant bee disappearing in the mist of the ocean water.

Story #2 (Version 4)
1. **Powerful**: I stood high on the hill, looking below at the crashing waves.
2. **Pleading**: Lucy walked up to me, grinning from ear to ear.
3. **Cheerful**: "I've been stung by a bumble bee," she said.
4. **Disbelieving**: She began to flail her arms and buzz like the bee that had stung her.
5. **Tense**: "Lucy," I called to her, "stop acting crazy."
6. **Amazed**: She didn't hear me; she didn't want to hear me.
7. **Disgusted**: She flew off the hill, towards the crashing waves.
8. **Happy**: And as she did, all I saw was a giant bee disappearing in the mist of the ocean water.

Story #2 (Version 5)
1. **Happy**: I stood high on the hill, looking below at the crashing waves.
2. **Stupid**: Lucy walked up to me, grinning from ear to ear.
3. **Energetic**: "I've been stung by a bumble bee," she said.
4. **Nervous**: She began to flail her arms and buzz like the bee that had stung her.
5. **Powerful**: "Lucy," I called to her, "stop acting crazy."

6. **Shocked**: She didn't hear me; she didn't want to hear me.
7. **Silly**: She flew off the hill, towards the crashing waves.
8. **Angry**: And as she did, all I saw was a giant bee disappearing in the mist of the ocean water.

Story #2 (Version 6)

1. **Shocked**: I stood high on the hill, looking below at the crashing waves.
2. **Determined**: Lucy walked up to me, grinning from ear to ear.
3. **Paranoid**: "I've been stung by a bumble bee," she said.
4. **Excited**: She began to flail her arms and buzz like the bee that had stung her.
5. **Hateful**: "Lucy," I called to her, "stop acting crazy."
6. **Pleading**: She didn't hear me; she didn't want to hear me.
7. **Frustrated**: She flew off the hill, towards the crashing waves.
8. **Terrified**: And as she did, all I saw was a giant bee disappearing in the mist of the ocean water.

SECTIONS III-IV: A FINAL NOTE

While it's recommended—if not imperative—that students perform all or most of the exercises in Section 1 before moving ahead, it is not the same for the improvisational sections. It's not as if I have my students perform all 102 improvisations and 19 group improvisations in the same time period. I spread them out over many months, from the beginning of the year till the end, because I believe improvisation should be a regular activity once it is introduced, understood and enjoyed by the students.

<u>Improvisation Contest</u>

Here's something you may want to try if you have multiple classes: I have, for many years, held improvisation contests between my two beginning drama classes. It's an event that lasts 2-3 hours and includes scores for each individual improvisation. Typically I have more than 70 chairs on stage occupied by students (and that's not counting the many students who stand). It has become a popular annual event at my school, and it's a great way to promote drama and keep students engaged and interested. If you're going to have a drama program, you are going to need a dedicated, engaged group of students.

Students from each class perform the same improvisation, taking turns which side performs first. For each improvisation, I—with the input of advanced students—give each class a score out of a possible total 10 points. I choose improvisations familiar to students, those that they had already done in their classes with fairly good success.

On the following page, I've included what a scorecard might look like.

Improvisation	Period 4	Period 5
Car Mimic	8.0	7.5
Emotion Arms	7.5	8.5
Gibberish Translation	9.0	8.0
Gibberish Mimics	8.5	7.5
Environment Switches	8.0	8.5
Rhyme Stories	7.0	8.0
Freeze Tags	7.5	9.0
Word Tennis	8.0	8.5
Imaginary Props	9.0	8.5
Genre Pairs	9.0	9.0
Total Score	**81.5**	**83.0**

SECTION V:
Beyond Assignments

SECTION V: FOREWARD

When I referred to the "Beyond" stage earlier in the book, I was thinking specifically about these assignments. Not only do they require extended planning and practice on the students' parts, they should only be performed when the prerequisites, particularly those exercises in Section 1, have been completed. Many of the assignments are natural progressions of exercises, dialogues or improvisations.

Though a couple of them may be categorized as foundational, the majority of them are creative and challenging. They represent a large pool of assignments from which I draw from. I have, at some point in time, given these assignments to my students. Some I give every year, because they are tried and true. Others I have given, though perhaps not every year. Much depends on the ability of my students and the time available during the year. For instance, if I have a class that is exceptional at improvisation and scripted scene work, I may do more of those activities. If a have a group that works well in teams, planning group scenes, I may favor those more. Ideally, I like to do everything from Sections 1-4. In any case, I will describe the many long-range, creative assignments that have been successful for my students and me. In addition, I will indicate where and when these assignments might be placed, in relation to prior classroom exercises and activities.

SPEECH

Foundational Speaking Practice

I give this assignment to my students shortly after—or sometimes before—finishing Section 1 warm ups and exercises. Although I call this one "Foundational Speaking Practice," the reality is that everything my students do throughout the year, with the exception of a pantomime assignment, is a variation of foundational speaking practice, since they are novices in the skill and art of speaking. Superficially, the assignment is called a speech. Fundamentally, it is an extended exercise, incorporating the same kind of verbal, vocal, and pronunciation drills used in Section 1. The critical difference is that here students perform individually. The assignment asks that they write a simple one-minute speech, either presenting or accepting an award. I will provide sample written speeches, along with guidelines, about how to organize and write them, but first I need to discuss the essential part of the assignment—how it should be delivered.

I want them, at all times, to exaggerate their delivery, for the objective is for them to speak with clarity, exactness and control. To accomplish these goals, they must do the following: They must slow their rate, unnaturally, in an exaggerated way. They must stretch their vowels and strike their consonants in exaggerated ways. They must open their mouths, move their jaws and use their tongues on their palates in exaggerated ways. They must recall the many exercises in Section 1, aimed at training them to respect sounds, syllables and words. In other words, they must learn to speak.

You may be aware that I have not used the word "talking" interchangeably with "speaking." Here's the reason: anyone can talk; it requires little more than a lazy opening of the mouth—a nearly automatic mechanical response—to produce sounds, though they may be incoherent and unclear. Talking may be acceptable for everyday life activities, such as hanging out with friends, mumbling exchanges to one another. This type of talking, however, is unacceptable for drama.

Speaking, on the other hand, requires motivation and effort. It requires energy, control and awareness. It requires a consciousness and a will to communicate. It requires a sense of purpose. Most of all, it requires practice. Therefore, in the context of my drama class, I avoid the word "talking." I use only "speaking" because it is positive, assertive and authoritative. With that said, I will now move on to the mechanical component of the assignment—the writing of the speech, as it might appear to the students.

Directions:

For this assignment, each student works with a partner. One gives a presentation speech, and the other gives an acceptance speech. The presenter gives an award to someone who has done a good deed. The person receiving the award speaks about what the award means to him.

How to begin:

The students should decide who will present and who will accept. In addition, they should help each other follow the directions and write the speeches.

Directions for Writing the Presentation Speech:
(sample speech *italicized*)

1. Make a remark about why the audience is attending the occasion:
   > *Good morning, ladies and gentlemen. Welcome to our annual Good Samaritan Award Ceremony.*

2. Name the person you are honoring, and explain why you are honoring him:
   > *Today we are honoring Roberto Salazar for his contributions to our community.*

3. Describe the good deeds the person performed:
   > *Although only 17 years old, Roberto has made a positive impact on those he meets, both in and out*

of school. This past year, he volunteered at a homeless shelter and helped many people and families recover from their hardships. Many times he sacrificed his own lunch or meals to help others more unfortunate than him. He has befriended one individual in particular, providing this man with a sleeping bag, shoes and socks and, most importantly, conversation and human kindness. As a student, he works in an after-school program, where he teaches small children, native to his own language and culture, to read and write in English. He truly understands what it means to give back to his friends and family, and those in his community.

4. Present the award to the winner.
    Ladies and gentlemen, it is with great pleasure that I give this Good Samaritan Award to Roberto Salazar.

Directions for Writing the Acceptance Speech:
(sample speech *italicized*)

1. Express gratitude (appreciation) for the award:
    Thank you, Mr. Smiley. I am very pleased to accept this award.

2. Recall an anecdote about someone who influenced you to perform the good deeds:
    I give credit to my grandmother. She has been my influence, the reason for my motivation in all areas of my life. When I was young, we were very poor, but she used to say, "It's not how much you have in your bank account, it's how much you have in your heart that matters. If you give to people, you will be a rich person.

3. Express what the award means to you, and how it will affect your future goals:
    I am indeed a rich person. It is only through help-

ing others that life has meaning. I will continue to volunteer my time, and I will work hard in school to reach my goal. I want to become a doctor, so I can help people in poor countries. I want to do it for myself, but more importantly, I want to do it for the legacy of giving my grandmother passed on to me.

4. Write and say a final thank you:
> *Once again, I want to thank everyone who voted for me to win this award.*

As you can see, the writing of the assignment is fairly simple. In fact, it's purposefully simple so that students can concentrate more on their delivery, satisfying the all-important speaking component of the assignment. Once they've written the speech—and this usually takes one class period—I monitor their practice. They divide into pairs, and the first thing they do is memorize their speeches. This is an essential requirement. I do not allow them to use a paper to read when they perform. They will not use papers later on when they perform dialogues and scenes from scripts. I want them to develop strong memorization skills. Besides, reading from a paper does not constitute the proper way to give a speech. A speech must be communicated to an audience. To satisfy this communication, students must memorize their words and express them in accordance with the assignment.

Here, then, are the standards I want them to achieve:

- Slow (exaggerated) rate
- Sharp as a razor clear
- Acceptable volume
- Complete memorization
- Direct communication with audience

Just as I did with the many exercises in Section 1, I model the desired expectations. (Note: I do not, at any time in this book, suggest how to grade. I attempt to explain the standards and guidelines of each exercise, improvisation and assignment. That should suffice):

> *Good evening...ladies...and...gentlemen...*
> *Welcome...to the annual...Good Samaritan...*
> *Award...Ceremony.*

The ellipsis indicates that the rate I use is unnaturally slow. This is not an exercise about fluency and rhythm. It's about clarity and control. I use the proper mechanics of my mouth, lips, tongue and jaw to emphasize my pronunciation in an exaggerated way, following through on every consonant. I am not in a rush. I enjoy the sound of syllables and words.

When my students perform I monitor closely. If one of them speeds the rate, gets lazy and mumbles, I stop him. Realistically, I can't stop every line that each of my 36 students speak, but I can have individual students repeat certain lines in their speeches and mimic—in part—what I modeled for them. The point is they must learn to be clear and exact, with enough volume. While a few students come to me with a natural gift for speaking, most do not. They need training. If I stop and re-direct them in the beginning of the year, it will pay dividends later. If I train them well, a time will come when they begin to speak better and move beyond fundamental speaking practice. Still, speaking clearly can never be taken for granted. Students always need exercises to make themselves ready to speak.

MONOLOGUES

1. Exploring Emotions in a Soliloquy

Many of the exercises in Section 1 and many of the dialogues in Section 2 are designed to help students stretch their emotional ranges. Some of my assignments, such as this one, become an extension of those exercises. Though the assignment is contrived and formulaic, it has long-range benefits. After a while, students will not need formulas to access emotional ranges. This is an assignment I will give to students two weeks before I expect them to perform it. The two weeks gives them sufficient time to write their soliloquy, memorize it, and practice it. After the instructions, I include a sample soliloquy wherein the student indicates on his script his changing emotional state. Here are the directions as they are written for the students:

Write out and prepare/perform a two-minute emotional-exploration soliloquy. Choose four (contrasting) emotions from the list below and use them in a remembrance story that is fictional. Do not communicate a personal remembrance. Drama class should not be confused with therapy. Whatever you do should be natural and believable. You don't need fancy staging for this exercise. You might want to use a prop or two. What's important in a soliloquy are your eyes and how you process your feelings. We often feel something and show it non-verbally before we use words to express it. In a remembrance circumstance, images are critical. If you see the image, the audience shares in the experience.

Take your time. Pauses are essential. They show that you're processing, understanding, struggling, realizing, discovering, etc. This exercise is not about words. It's about communicating emotions. When you switch emotions, make sure you switch to a feeling that is dramatically different from the previous one. Even though you're following a contrived formula here, your transitions from emotion to emotion should appear and sound seamless and natural. Communicating emotions (listed below) naturally and under control is an essential component of performing drama believably:

Anxious	Kind	Indecisive	Afraid
Timid	Tense	Smart	Cunning
Terrified	Pleading	Impatient	Nervous
Tragic	Arrogant	Enthusiastic	Frustrated
Angry	Nasty	Exhausted	Fearful
Confident	Yearning	Sickly	Coy
Stubborn	Exasperated	Suspicious	Combative
Joyful	Disgusted	Sad	Happy
Determined	Mean	Amused	Doubtful
Amazed	Bitter	Worried	Mischievous
Bossy	Bored	Disbelieving	Sly
Loving	Hesitant	Melancholic	Excited
Gentle	Peaceful	Triumphant	Cheerful
Shocked	Irritated	Powerful	Careless
Annoyed	Embarrassed	Ambitious	Compliant

Sample Emotional Monologue:

(Calm) *A happy memory? You wish to know a happy memory of mine? Sure.* (Pause. Subtle Happiness) *Christmas Day, one of the happiest days of the year.* (Pause) *I was ten years old that day. It started when my family arrived at my Aunt's house. My entire family was there: my uncles, cousins, and grandparents. Everyone was happy and having a good time. My grandfather was telling my uncles his army stories. My cousins were playing, and my little sister was helping to cook dinner by banging two pots together.* (Annoyed) *Stupid. She was six years old and acted like she was two.* (Pause) *After a while my mom came out and announced that dinner was ready.*

(Excitement) *What a feast! There were turkey, bread, corn, and white, pillowy mashed potatoes* (Pause, sees the potatoes) *so thick you just wanted to sleep in them like they were clouds. Just add some gravy and you find yourself* (Pause, takes bites) *in heaven.*

After dinner all I wanted to do was open my presents. I was getting impatient, and my grandfather could tell. He came over to talk to me. (Annoyed, bored) *At first he was asking me the boring stuff: How am I? How is school? Do I like any girls? Boring, boring, boring. I was too old for those questions. I was a big kid, nearly ten, and I asked him something I'd been dying to know. I looked into his great old wrinkly eyes and asked, "Grandpa, what was the war like?" Those eyes which were usually filled with warmth and happiness now became distant and dark.* (Horror, Scared) *He began to tell me about that day on the beach, the horrors he saw, men screaming and getting killed. Blood-soaked sand, body parts everywhere. He said he had never before experienced so much fear.*

(Sad) *I found myself staring at him. His eyes started to tear.* (Pause) *Behind me I heard the footsteps of my grandmother. She gently laid her hand on my shoulder and kneeled down to whisper into my ear.* (Excited) *Presents! It was about time since grandpa was becoming such a buzz kill. I raced to the living room, leaving my weeping grandfather behind. When I got to the living room, everyone was there, and they were gathered around the fire.* (Amazed) *I saw the largest, most magnificent pile of gifts I'd ever seen in my life. I was getting ready to dive into the pile and swim through all those gifts, but then* (Shift to Annoyance) *asked my little sister to hand out each present, one by one, to everyone. Once again, my "cute" little sister was getting between me and what I wanted.*

(Return to Excitement) *But soon enough my turn came. My sister handed me some envelopes. I could feel my heart ready to jump out of my chest. I quickly ripped the edges of each one and dumped the contents in my lap.* (Explosion of Happiness) *Money!!! Yes!!! The greatest of gifts! I touched the money, smelled the money. I wanted to eat the money. Now I was truly happy—or so I thought.*

(Jealous) *My sister also received money, and she was waving it around, acting awfully cute as she did it. I was wondering if she got more money than me, on account of her being a girl, and being so cute. Life seemed so unfair at that moment.*

(Intense, with an Idea) *As she was waving her money*

around she waddled her little butt closer and closer to the fireplace. (Shocked) *Then she did the unimaginable. She threw her money in the fireplace.* (Anger) *That little...how dare she do that? That money could have been mine.* (Demonic, Possessed) *Full of rage, I walked up to her, turned her around and looked into her insipid little eyes.* (Even Crazier) *You like to throw things into the fire, do you? I said. Then I gripped her shoulders tighter and in a fit of insanity I threw her into the fire, and slammed the glass shutters closed.*

(Calm, Weirdly so) *And for some reason my family didn't take that too well. Now I'm here.* (Smiles) *With you.*

2. Monologue Using Actions/Physical Score

Here is another self-written monologue. While the Emotional Evolve monologue was all about expressing emotions, this one has a heavy concentration on actions. The emotion must be, of course, urgent and purposeful, as it should be in a monologue, but it has to be written, as well, as a "doing" monologue. The Emotional Evolve could be done sitting down. This one requires movement. It requires a marriage between words and actions.

What's Needed?
- Create a character and situation.
- Write a monologue (including a physical score) with urgent, purposeful emotion.
- Coordinate the monologue with actions and behavior that allows for
- A visual extension of the emotion.

Directions:

1. Use your imagination as far as what kind of character you can create, what kind of situation/emotion, what type of actions and behavior would best help illustrate the emotion of the story.
2. The monologue must have purpose. It's not inci-

216

dental. It's significant. The actions are important extensions of the emotions. Keep in mind that we—the audience—are influenced as much (probably more) by what we see as well as by what we hear.

3. You are required to type your monologue, indicating your actions.

The following is an example of a Monologue Using Actions/Phuysical Score:

"Roger opens the door, walks in, looks around and moans. He takes his jacket off, attempts to put it on the coat hanger, but misses (the jacket falls). He looks at it on the floor, considers picking it up, then decides to leave it on the floor. He speaks: "That was the worst movie I've ever seen. How could I have taken Sharon to such a rotten film on our first date? I'm such a jerk!" He slaps his head on the word "jerk."

He sits down on the couch, which is littered with yesterday's newspaper. He starts tearing one of the loose pages as he says, "She hated it, she hated it, she hated it," coordinating the tearing with the word "hated." He begins to untie his shoes and take them off. He says: "I'm so stupid...so stupid," coordinating the word "stupid" with the slamming down of each shoe. He gets up, walks over to the kitchen table, where an open box of cereal is placed next to a bowl and spoon. He sits and begins pouring cereal into the bowl. He eats the cereal dry and crunches loudly. He says (while crunching the cereal): "I'll never get another date with anyone. I'm such a loser."

He swallows, looks up, and realizes something. He says: "I should have taken her to a restaurant, she was probably hungry." He considers this last comment, then says: "But it's too late now. She'll never want to see me again. Never... never...never..."

He coordinates the word "never" with the tapping of his spoon on the table. He looks up, has another realization. He says: "Do I ever dare call her again?" He gets up, paces, and says: "Is it possible she doesn't hate me as much as I think she does?"

He rushes over to the couch, sits and lifts the phone receiver (placed on the table next to the couch). He begins dialing, then suddenly slams the receiver down. He says: "No, I know she hates me...she has to...doesn't she?" He considers this last comment. "I'll write her a letter, that's what I'll do." He gets up and crosses to his desk, where he sits and takes out paper and a pen. "Dear Sharon" he writes and says. "Dear Sharon" he writes and says again, more hesitantly. "Oh, what's the use?" He crumples the paper and tosses it in the air. "What's the use?"

He buries his head on his arms atop the table. He lifts his head suddenly, excited for a moment. "Someone once told me, 'Feel the fear, but do it anyway'," he says. He gets up. "That's what I'm going to do. Feel the fear, but do it anyway. Where's that phone?"

He crosses again to the couch, sits and dials Sharon's number. "Hello, Sharon.

Yeah, this is Roger. R-O-G-E-R...why am I calling? Because I've decided to feel the fear, but do it anyway. Sharon?...Are you still there? Sharon?" He hangs up the phone and dejectedly sits back on the couch. "She hung up on me. I can't believe it. Oh, woe is me. I'll never love again." He collapses, lying down. (Monologue ends.)"

3. Monologue Using Music

Here is a way to combine speaking, actions and music. It is a challenging assignment, but definitely worth employing to get students to understand the relationship between music, language and actions. Here's the directions I give the students:

Create a character and write a monologue, and, at the same time, find a piece of instrumental music. Practice speaking with the music. Select music that changes moods, rhythms, tones and tempos, allowing for the monologue to shift and change accordingly. Of course, your nonverbal expressions should also change as the music shifts. It may work better for you to first find music and suit the character and words to it. Nonetheless, your objective here is to coordinate your spoken word and actions to your selected music. The minimum time frame is two minutes.

4. Monologue From a Play/Book

A monologue is a speech of some length given by one character. It is addressed to one or more characters on stage. A soliloquy is a speech of some length given by someone who is alone on stage. In this speech, the actor reveals his thoughts and feelings to the audience. Monologues/Soliloquies are reflections, confessions (emotional journeys), revealing the needs and urgencies of characters; they are showstoppers, riveting the audience's attention to a specific moment in time and space.

Perform a minimum two-minute monologue/soliloquy. You can find monologues in novels, plays, or monologue books (I have a collection you can look through). Find one that suits you physically, psychologically and emotionally. Do not write your own. As well as practicing and performing your monologue, you will need to type out a Physical Score (a detail-by-detail account of movement/actions that supplement the words) and a Character Biography. In addition, you will need to—on a separate sheet—answer the following questions, designed to help you understand what you're speaking:

1. What is the environment/setting/background for this monologue?
2. What is the "moment before?" In other words, where are you coming from? Where have you been? What did you just do before you started speaking? (You should approach it as if you're in the middle of something, not at the beginning.)
3. What is the purpose of your speech? What is your motive/objective? Who are you talking to? What is your urgency or need?
4. What is the complexity of emotions that you're feeling? (You should break your script down by units of emotion.)
5. What are the struggles and/or conflicts your character faces?

Additional Notes

- Begin your speech with energy and purpose; appear as someone who has something important to communicate.
- Pick a monologue that will make you perform and move, not merely talk. Suit your actions to your words. Remember, "an ounce of behavior is worth a pound of words."
- Strive for spontaneity. It should look and sound like you're performing for the first time.
- Recall the Emotional Evolve Monologue from earlier in the year. Discover and communicate your full emotional range.
- If you're performing a monologue, look at your imaginary partner sparingly. See the images you are recalling. If you believe you see them, the audience will likewise believe.
- Don't rush. Often, in life, we see, sense or feel something before we say it.
- Though you are memorizing words, you must talk, move and act in a natural, believable way. It's called Acting.

SCENES FOR TWO PEOPLE

1. Actions and Behaviors

This scene/assignment is really just an exercise in creating character, relationship, status, conflict, etc. through your behavior and actions (by doing very little, in fact). The focus will not be so much on what you do, but rather on "how" you do it.

Write a script, following the one-step-at-a-time format below, using words sparingly, perhaps 20% of your scene, at most. The majority of the scene should include stage directions which reveal movements and behaviorisms: the tilt of your head, the shift or steady glare of your eyes, the caress of your hand, the blow of smoke from the cigarette you smoke, the wipe of your brow, etc.

This scene need not be long, three minutes is sufficient. Of course, as in any scene, you need a story in which two people are in a real environment for a specific purpose. Use an environment that is simple. Almost any setting can work if the behaviorisms are detailed and specific. The story itself need not be complete. It can be a moment, a fragmentary one, as long as it's intriguing, mysterious, and psychologically stimulating.

To introduce this assignment, I typically read the following example, while two students act it out. Afterwards, I give each student a copy of the script.

Detailed, Moment-by-Moment Scene:

Joan sits, waiting at a bus stop.
She is on her way to an important interview.
She is looking through her wallet for an address she needs.
She is frustrated because she can't find the address.
Also, the bus is late.
James approaches. He studies the bus schedule, left of where Joan sits.
He then turns and looks at Joan.

A moment later, he sits next to her, continuing to look at her.

Joan does not look up. She remains focused on her wallet's contents.

James leans back and studies Joan's movements.

Joan, suspecting she is being watched, shuts her wallet.

She then stands and moves to the bus schedule, examining it.

She checks her watch.

James leans forward, in her direction. He says, "Excuse me, do you have the time?"

Joan turns to him. She studies his face a moment before speaking.

"9:05," she says. She paces a few steps, stops and sighs.

She takes out a folder and reviews some notes.

James leans back again, this time crossing his legs. He continues to stare at Joan.

He takes a piece of gum out of his shirt pocket, unwrapping it slowly.

He begins chewing the gum, loudly.

He takes another piece of gum from his pocket. He holds it out in Joan's direction.

"Wanna piece of gum?" He says.

Joan does not look at him.

She says, "No thank you."

"Are you sure?" He says. "It's cinnamon."

He pauses, smiles. "You're favorite," he says.

Joan turns suddenly.

Their eyes lock.

In Drama, as revealed in the above scene, less if often times more. Although there are few words spoken between the two people, a great deal seems to be going on, conveyed through the actions and behaviorisms of the actors. A relationship—albeit a mysterious one—takes shape. The audience can only infer (guess) about their motives. The emphasis on actions and behaviors, rather than words, stimulates our imaginations.

2. Scene in Rhyme

Rhyme is something I do quite a bit in repeats and improvisations, but I also like to have my students write a scene
in rhyme. The reason is this: most students have trouble
coming up with rhymes improvisationally, but, if given
time, they can write, and then perform, imaginative, clever
scenes. Here's what I give them.

You and a partner will create a scene, written and performed in rhyme. Although rhyme schemes vary, the best
one for this assignment would be rhyme in couplets
(consecutive lines that rhyme). You can vary the patterns
you use. For instance, one person can start a line and have
it completed by the other person. Or one person can speak,
using a couplet, followed by the other using a couplet. The
best approach might be using a combination of different
patterns, as long as the dialogue rhymes. Each pair will receive a packet that includes rhyme sounds in the most
common sounds (a, e, i, o, u). Use this packet to help you
include a variety of words and sounds.

The scene, otherwise, should follow the standards of any
scene. You must create characters in a specific situation,
with the usual components of a drama-related scene: story,
relationship, conflict, emotion, suspense, etc.

When you speak in rhyme, you must accentuate/stress
the rhyme sounds. It doesn't mean you have to speak nonstop from beginning to end. You could (and should, as in
any scene) have pauses and actions that accompany the
words you speak. You will, of course, need to write out a
script, then rehearse/practice appropriately.

In place of providing an example, I offer the following
brief excerpt of a scene written by two students:

Characters:
- Captain Apache, a tough, stern pirate in search of a
  certain treasure.
- Brutus, a pirate who lives in servitude to Captain
  Apache.

223

The main deck of Captain Apache's ship.

Example Script:

Brutus:	*Captain, there's something I need to tell you.* *Something very important in my view.*
Apache:	*Brutus, now is not the time.* *Do your job, removing the ship's rime.*
Brutus:	*But, Captain, you really must know* *That someday I would like to go.*
Apache:	*Go, Brutus? Go where?* *As I am your Captain, you wouldn't dare.* *To me and my ship, you are under servtude.* *Now, get to work, no more foolish attitude.*
Brutus:	*Forgive me, my Captain, but I had a wonderful dream.* *Something unforgettable did happen, it may seem.*
Apache:	*It's interesting how you seem bold.* *Usually you're shy and you're thoughts are untold.*
Brutus:	*In my dream, I saw myself brave.* *Pursuing the new profession I crave.* *You see, I've fallen in love with poetry.* *A great writer, suddenly, is what I want to be.*

This scene has a good beginning. It establishes a location, two characters, in a specific relationship to one another, and a conflict. And it's also written in couplets.

3. Script From a Play

Here's how I tell students to approach this exercise:

Find a scene from a play (Approximate time length: 5-10 minutes). If you want your scene to be successful, choose one that's appealing, accessible, engaging—ideally, one that requires staging (a visual component). Avoid a "talking heads" scene. After you have your scene and make a copy of it, always bring it to class. Here's the most effective way to approach working on a scene:

Stage 1: Read and analyze

The script will provide you with words. That's all. You need to analyze (discuss) why you're character is saying and doing what she's saying and doing. You'll need to use your imaginations to supply what's missing from the script. Make decisions (choices) about who the characters are and why they're engaged with each other, in that specific setting/situation. Write freely and thoughtfully on your scripts, reflecting your on-going analysis and your staging notes. Here are some succinct, critical acting comments:

1. Acting is an art form that requires invention on the part of the performers.
2. Acting involves listening and watching; reacting and behaving believably.
3. Every movement (action) has a purpose; every moment is significant.
4. Specific detail engages an audience. If you can control each movement, each action, each word, each detail, each "beat" in the script—my gosh, you will satisfy the artistic requirement in the process of acting.

Stage 2: Moving, staging, and positioning ("Blocking)

If you understand the character emotions and relations, you should be able to convey them through standing, sitting, crossing, etc. Proximity is very important. The distance between characters often depends on the relationship and mood of the scene. During this stage you should use props (tables, doors, chairs, etc.) to help you find the right positions.

You need to slow down during this stage. Write out and practice a physical score, where you can account for each action and have purposeful detail throughout the scene.

Throughout stages 1 and 2 you must consciously employ speaking techniques. What do you want to emphasize? Where do you want to pause? When do you speed up or slow down? What kind of texture or quality do you want to give your voice? Speaking language is like playing music. It must be practiced and rehearsed. You must continuously improvise and experiment with your words and voices to discover the desired sound/effect.

For the performance of your scene, use appropriate costumes, props and scenery. These necessary elements make an immediate impression on your audience, communicating whether you are serious about your work.

(Note: For scenes and monologues from plays and books, I do have my students complete a Character Biography. Sometimes I have them write it out in essay form.) Other times, I have them complete the sheet I've included on the following page:

Character Biography
Character name:
Actor's name:

Physical Detail
Age:
Posture:
Mannerisms:
Voice quality:
Appearance:

Psychological/Behavioral
Regrets:
Secrets:
Prejudices:
Curiosities:
Self-Image:

Social Nature
Education:
Family:
Relationships:
Friends:
Love Life:

Philosophies
Religious views:
Hopes, Fears, Dreams:
Interests/Passions:
Attitude:

GROUP SCENES

9. Genre Scene

Before I give this assignment, I know my students have engaged in numerous genre activities, including exercises and improvisations. For this one—to put it simply—they choose a genre and create a scene, approximately 5-7 minutes in length. This one can be either short-term or long-term, depending on the type of students I have. If it's short-term, I have them plan it for a day, and then develop it improvisationally as they perform the next day. If it's long-term, I'll have them write a script. Typically, advanced students are more capable of the long-term scene, and beginning students are more likely to perform the short-term version. Again, it depends on who's in your class. In any case, whether it's short-term or long-term, I give my students similar guidelines for creating setting, relationship and storyline. Anytime they plan and perform a scene of length, I want them to follow the standard Dramatic Plot Structure, which I outline here:

1. Start with Exposition. Establish the time, place, characters, relationships and themes.
2. Present the Initial Incident. Something happens to introduce conflict.
3. Make sure there's Rising Action. This includes a series of actions that builds tension and suspense.
4. Progress towards a Climax. Here is the moment of highest intensity, when a decision must be made.
5. Follow the Climax with Falling Action. This phase of the story's development reveals the results of the prior climactic decisions. Finally the scene ends in a resolution.

While I wrote earlier, that I was not going to address grading practices, I will, however, write down my performance standards. These standards apply to all scenes my students perform throughout the year:

- Focus/Concentration (completely in the moment)
- Believability/Conviction (audience believes that you believe)
- Expressive Voice (dramatic clarity, emotion & meaning)
- Characterization (suggestion through voice, body, movement)
- Staging/Blocking (well-balanced, well-presented visual composition)
- Relationship (the essence of all drama)
- Energy/Presence (the ability to make an audience pay attention to you)
- Motivation (your purpose for saying what you say and doing what you do)
- Costume/Props (aids in establishing believability and trustworthiness)

Here, finally, is the list of genres I give them:

Spy thriller	Musical comedy
Mystery thriller	Action thriller
Opera	Hip hop
Soap opera	Children's story
Country western	Fairy tale
Romance	Fable
Hillbilly	Detective
Supernatural	Surfer
Horror	Fantasy
Sea adventure	Ethnic/accent
Cartoon	Melodrama
Shakespearean	Tragedy
Foreign	Classical

10. Musical Comedy Scene

Here's a variation of the previous scene. It's still a genre scene. The difference is that I make this one a musical genre. It's not a scene I assign every year, but if I feel I have enough students who can sing—or who are willing to sing—it's a good choice. For this scene, I have to give the students extra time, perhaps 10 days, because they need to write a script that includes song lyrics. It's a creative, challenging scene. Anyway, here's what I tell the students:

"Each group will be performing a musical scene in a different genre. Whatever the genre, consider the following characteristics of a musical scene:"

1. There must be a mix of dialogue and singing
2. There are always "high stakes" moments
3. The tone/mood of a musical scene involves heightened "emotionalism."

"Now, I realize most of you are not blessed with great singing voices. Neither am I. Just have fun creating dialogue, lyrics and songs. While you can model your scene and songs on existing musicals and music, your words, songs and dialogue should be original. Strive to have a balance between dialogue and songs. As well as focusing on the lyrics and singing, find ways to make the scene visually pleasing. Consider lights, costumes, props, etc. Even though you are mostly creating and developing a moment in a musical, do your best to frame the scene with a solid beginning, middle and end. I'm assuming your scenes will be approximately 15 minutes long."

What's needed?
- A typed script
- Original song lyrics
- A list of genres (refer to the list from the previous assignment)

11. Situations and Characters

The scene does not have to be performed in a genre. Sometimes I give each group a situation with characters and have them create a musical based on this information. Of course, I can—and usually do—give this assignment as a straight scene, without the musical element. In any case, the scene, like most long-range, group scenes, will most likely need to be scripted and planned out. I write "most likely" only because it can also be performed as a short-range scene, without script. Whichever format used, here are the situations and characters I give to the groups:

<u>Family Scene:</u>
> *A guest arrives. It could be an old friend, a relative, a sibling, a husband, wife, etc. The arrival of this person disturbs the family dynamic/balance. Approach it gradually and make sure each of the characters and their relationships to one another are developed. You decide whether it's comic, serious or a combination of both. Feel free to modify accordingly.*

   ➤ <u>Suggested characters:</u>
father, mother, sons, daughters, aunts, uncles, friend of the family

<u>Office Scene:</u>
> *A business/company is suffering due to economic hardships. Critical decisions have to be made. These decisions will have a ripple down effect on the entire staff. Approach it gradually and make sure each of the characters and their relationships to one another are developed. You decide whether it's comic, serious or a combination of both. Feel free to modify accordingly.*

   ➤ <u>Suggested characters:</u>
CEO, High Management, Accountant, Secretarial staff, Company lawyer, Mailroom employee, etc.

<u>Hotel/Restaurant Scene:</u>
> *It's business as usual in this high-class restaurant until an unexpected problem arises. This problem*

affects everyone in the restaurant. Approach it gradually and make sure each of the characters and their relationships to one another are developed. You decide whether it's comic, serious or a combination of both. Feel free to modify accordingly.

➤ <u>Suggested characters:</u>
romantic couple on their wedding anniversary, other customers, busboy, waiter/waitress, manager, etc.

<u>Hospital Scene:</u>
A person is brought to the emergency room one evening. Complications and misunderstandings arise between staff members, doctors, family members, etc. Approach it gradually and make sure each of the characters and their relationships to one another are developed. You decide whether it's comic, serious or a combination of both. Feel free to modify accordingly.

➤ <u>Suggested characters:</u>
doctors, nurses, patients, family members, police officer, etc.

<u>School/Classroom Scene:</u>
A conflict at school needs to be resolved before it becomes out of control. Take your time in introducing the conflict. First establish the characters and their relationships to one another. You decide whether the scene is comic, serious or a combination of both. Feel free to modify accordingly.

➤ <u>Suggested characters:</u>
teacher, counselor, administrator, parent, students

<u>Las Vegas Hotel Room:</u>
It's business as usual at this high-class resort hotel

until a problem arises over a mix up with rooms.
Take your time in introducing the problem. First
establish the characters their relationship to one
another. You decide whether the scene is comic, se-
rious or a combination of both. Feel free to modify
accordingly.

➤ Suggested characters:
  couple on vacation, single man or woman, maid,
  casino worker, management, etc.

12. Tall Tale Scene

Here is another large group scene that I always have my
students perform during the early part of the year. This one
could have been placed in Section 3 because I've seen it
performed both as short-range and long-range assignments. Which one I choose depends on the types my
students have been engaged in prior to this one. For
instance, if they recently completed a long-range, large-
group scene that included writing a script, I may choose to
have them perform this one with limited planning (more
improvisational). Conversely, if I haven't given any large-
group scenes that require writing and planning, I will
choose the long-range format. Either way, it is an engaging
assignment that I recommend highly. The information I
give the students is as follows:

A Tall Tale is a fib, a lie, a fabrication, an exaggeration,
but more than anything, it is entertaining. No limitations
exist in the telling/performing of the Tall Tale, as long as
you tell it/perform it in a believable way. Your group will
choose, from the list below, a commonly known object. You
will present a Tall Tale about how that particular object
came to be known to mankind. This one should have a
"Once upon a time" quality to it. You will need costumes
and props to convey the magic and exaggeration of the tale.
A narrator, who can also play a role, is highly recommended for this one. Spend your time wisely. Plan it out so
that you have a magical, colorful, wonderfully fabricated—
and even unbelievably outrageous—tale.

Choose an object from the following list:

Flashlight	Fly swatter	Nose hair clipper
Flower	Nail clipper	Paint brush
Can opener	Pillow	Toothbrush
Floss	Lamp	Hair comb
Pot holder	Ring	Paper clip
Screwdriver	Belt	Backpack
Yo-yo	Hat	Rope
Pea	Hair clip	Pencil

13. Fairy Tale Adaptations

This one, like the previous one, requires students to adopt a "Once Upon a Time" approach. In fact, I want them to use a specific fairy tale. However, I don't want them to perform it verbatim or in its traditional context. I want them to play with the plot, the characters and the overall storyline. For example, they might use the "Hansel and Gretel" story, only their story takes place in the Dustbowl in Oklahoma, and the details of the story are very specific to the history of that time period. Or, perhaps their "Cinderella" story takes place in Russia, and the lead character is a male named Dimitri who lives under the oppressive rule of his father, a member of Joseph Stalin's Cabinet. Maybe the "Snow White" story takes place in Los Angeles, in a high fashion modeling industry where the top model is jealous of a new girl.

I'm providing examples I've seen in my classes. Students need to be inventive and clever in order to adopt effectively a well-known fairy tale. In addition to the information I've just stated, I provide the students with the following directions for performing a successful scene:

1. Planning Stage: Decide on the fairy tale you'll be adopting, and then write a script.
2. Acting Style: A Fairy Tale belongs in the "Unreal" genre. Therefore, you will need to stretch your vocal and physical ranges for this assignment.
3. You must be larger than life and appropriately

"affected". Alter your voices and create specific physical characteristics.

4. Costumes & Props: The scene cannot possibly succeed without inventive visuals.

5. How you embellish the characters and settings with costumes and props will determine audience interest and the all-important believability of the tale.

6. Practicing Stage: Though the planning stage is critical you want to make sure that the majority of your time is spent practicing on your feet, deciding on appropriate staging.

14. Holiday Scene

Here's one I like to do during the holiday season in December: What is a holiday scene? Well, it's a scene that centers on the holiday season, whatever that means to you. Typically, there is almost always an adverse situation that needs to be overcome. In the end, however, everything turns out right: "There is a Santa Claus!" or "Daddy, you're home!" or Mr. Scrooge re-evaluates what's important in life. While the outcomes are often predictable, the telling of the story doesn't (and shouldn't) have to be.

Of course, you don't have time to plan out and perform a two-hour movie script. Therefore, the challenge for your group will be to make creative, compelling choices with character development, character relationships and storylines, in a 12-15 minute scene. Here are the requirements:

1. Type out a script and practice attentively with one purpose in mind: to perform an effective scene that appropriately conveys the holiday season. Keep in mind that your scene reflects your script. A good script can become a good scene. A bad script gives you little or no chance to perform a good scene. Make sure your script covers the important bases. Beginnings are critical for establishing the who, what and where. Do not rush this critical part of the story structure. Make sure relationships between characters are developed. After all, relationships

are the heart of acting and the heart of all stories.

2. The visual part of a Holiday scene is as important as the story itself. These scenes especially need embellishments such as props, costumes and scenery. I guarantee these scenes will not be effective without these essential elements. Therefore, a significant part of your practice needs to address how you can make your scene look right. You must think about how you can integrate sound, lights, props and costumes.

EXPERIMENTAL SCENES

15. Three-Person Shared Soliloquy

As an alternative to the emotion soliloquy assignment I made for one person, I created a more experimental one, wherein three students play the same character and share the lines, story and emotions. In this format, the three students stand right, center and left on stage and tell the story one sentence at a time. I also encourage them to use overlap and speaking in unison, at times. This one, though experimental in its format, is, nonetheless, a soliloquy. It must reflect an emotional journey. To ensure that it's an emotional journey, I present it to them as a story with emotional shifts. I have them start by creating a compelling character, one with an urgency to tell his story. Here, then, is an example, approximately 4 minutes in length:

[The opening tone is reflective, a mix of seriousness, excitement and understatement.]

#1:   I remember that day, July 23rd, 1973, like it was yesterday.

#2:   (Pause) I was with my friends, canoeing on a river, in New Hampshire.

#3:   The sky was a brilliant blue, and the water was placid and friendly.

#1:   There were nine of us, in a total of three boats.

#2:   I was lucky enough to share my boat with my best friends.

#3:   Adonis and Cleopatra. How can I forget either of them?

#1:   Adonis was our leader, handsome, strong and fearless.

#2:   And Cleopatra was everything you would expect from someone...

#3:   ...with a name like Cleopatra. She was a princess supreme.

#1:   The truth is from the earliest ages each of them

seemed other worldly.

#2:   As if they weren't really meant for this world.

#3:   As if they belonged in a mythological world, with Gods.

#1:   I, on the other hand, was an ordinary Joe.

#2:   In fact, my name is Joe. Joseph Paul Colangeli.

#3:   Though the story I tell ... (pause) is far from ordinary.
        [The tone shifts to a mix of mysteriousness, sorrow and even tragedy.]

#1:   You see...(pause) ... that day ... (pause) Adonis and Cleopatra...

#2:   Did not return home with the rest of us.

#3:   (Pause) They did not drown in the waters of that river.

        [The tone shifts to a near craziness or madness, the result of too much sorrow.]

#1:   Oh, no! They definitely did not drown in the waters!

        [The tone shifts to a calm, seriousness.]

#2:   (Pause) They were taken.

#3:   (Pause) By whom or what, you may ask?

        [The tone shifts once again to a near craziness or madness, the result of pain.]

#1:   I will always believe, to this day, it was the Gods who took them!

#2:   Not the waters, definitely not the waters!

#3:   Those envious, ironic Gods that rule the underworld!

        [Pause. The tone becomes reflective, serious and matter of fact.]

#1:   Did I say underworld?

#2:   Oh, sure, they fell in the waters that day.
#3:   We all did.

[The tone shifts to a mix of madness and anger.]

#1:   But I floated to the surface.
#2:   As did the others.
#3:   In the other two boats.
#1:   How is it possible that Adonis and Cleopatra...
#2:   ...didn't come to the surface as well?

[Reaching a hysterical pitch.]

#3:   Where did they go?
#1:   Where did they go?
#2:   Where did they go?

[The tone is now quiet, nearly catatonic, as if in shock.]

#3:   They weren't in the waters, that much is certain.
#1:   The authorities search every inch of that river.

[Very mysterious now.]

#2:   The river was no more than ten feet deep.
#3:   You can find a gold fish in a ten-foot deep river.
#1:   So how is it that two bodies can't be found?

[A steely determination, with deep piercing, penetrating eyes.]

#2:   I'll tell you why they couldn't be found.
#3:   They were never meant for the world we inhabit.
#1:   They were returned to the mythology from whence they came.
#2:   To live as legends among the Gods.

[A burst of joy and happiness, though forced and irrational.]

#1:	Yes, that's what I believe...
#2:	And what I always will believe!
#3:	Because ... after all, why were they named
#1:	Adonis and Cleopatra in the first place?
#2:	Their very names are too big for this world we inhabit.
#3:	They were bestowed, at birth, with names like Gods.
#1:	So it stands to reason...
#2:	(Pause) Doesn't it?
#3:	That they would now...
#1:	...rest with the Gods.
#2:	Eternally.
#3:	Mythologically.

[Pause. The tone becomes reflective, as it was in the beginning, with a mix of resignation and the indestructible spirit of humanity.]

#1:	It's been 41 years since that day.
#2:	I have never returned to that river in New Hampshire.
#3:	And I have learned to carry on without my best friends.
#1:	I will soon turn 61 years old.
#2:	And as I live, I wait and wonder.
#3:	(Pause) Will the Gods come for me...
#1:	as they did for Adonis and Cleopatra?
#2:	Can a man with an ordinary name
#1:	like Joseph Paul Colangeli...
#2:	be included in the catalogue
#3:	of those who sit among the Gods?

16. Scene Plus Genres (for three students)

If you're looking for yet another type of genre assignment, this one tests students' abilities to stretch themselves vocally, verbally and nonverbally. Here are the instructions I give the students:

Write a dialogue that's no more than 45 seconds in length. Keep the scene simple in character and plot. The scene itself is little more than an exercise in genre and style. The interest comes from how you perform the scene, not necessarily in what the scene is about.

You will perform your simple script first, then two consecutive times, each in a different genre or style that you choose. While you don't have many lines to memorize, you will be challenged by how (specifically) you change the scene each time you perform it. You will need select props/objects/costume pieces, etc. to suggest each genre.

In choosing genres, look for contrasts from one to another. The tone and look of each successive scene should be contrasting.

Begin with a simple situation. Three people. Where are they? Who are they? What is happening? You're not expected to have a complete story. Quickly write/type a short script, then spend most of your time rehearsing the staging and changes. Keep in mind that each genre has a distinct look and sound. Your body language should be different in each change; your voice texture should be different.

17. Music Pantomime

The next three assignments are not large-group assignments. In fact, two of them are solo assignments, and one is a two-person scene. The one commonality is that in these assignments there is a greater concentration on actions and behavior.

In Section 1, I led my students through various pantomime activities. I sometimes assign a pantomime, much like the one called "42" Details. This one is a pantomime that asks students to coordinate actions and music. It is extremely challenging, but I have seen remarkable results with this assignment. Therefore, I am including it here, despite its sophistication. Here, then, are the instructions given to the students:

For this assignment, you're going to create/convey dramatic expression through the use of music (but don't confuse it with dance). You will start by choosing an instrumental piece of music that has dramatic, interpretive appeal. Allow the music to determine where you are and what you're doing/feeling. Create a character, a situation. What's important is that you coordinate your actions to the music that is being played.

You must choreograph your exercise moment by moment, musical note by musical note. It should not be busy. It should be controlled, focused, and concentrated. Aim for specific detail: the lift of a hand, the opening or closing of an eye, the disappearance or appearance of a smile, the opening or closing of a box, etc. The entire exercise can be performed in one contained space. You will not have words to speak; therefore, your facial expressions, your gestures, and your movements become the essential means of communication. Again, the challenge here is to coordinate these actions with the music. This exercise should be a minimum of 60 seconds.

18. Scene with a Soundtrack

In this scene you create a soundtrack for the script you write. Or you may decide to create a soundtrack first, and then write a script. Whichever invention you use, consider that music does not have to play continuously through the scene. Rather, the words and music can alternate. For instance, the scene starts with music playing. Someone walks in. Then the music stops, and the words are spoken. It might be best to use this format throughout since there would be no distraction when someone is talking. Whatever you do, you should use a variety of music because the tone and mood of the scene should keep changing.

I'm assuming students possess the "know how" and the smart technology in order to select and edit music accordingly. The idea of the scene is as follows: you create a spoken scene around the music that you find and use. In other words, the mood and tone of the scene changes as the music changes. Here's another way to state it: you are speaking and moving while music is playing in the background. Therefore, the planning of this scene has three components:

1. Find enough music for a five-minute scene. The music you use should be varied in tone and mood and should change every 20-30 seconds or thereabouts. The music dictates the scene. As the music changes, the tone and mood of the scene changes.
2. Write a script (after you have created your soundtrack). If you start with suspenseful music the script would begin in suspense. It may then switch to relaxed music, wherein the scene would then be relaxed in sound and tone and movement. Again, the music you use determines what you write and how you speak the words and, in fact, what you do on stage, in regards to movement and actions.
3. Rehearse attentively to coordinate all actions and words to the type of music that is playing in the background.

19. The Story of a Person's Life

This scene develops from one person's story. Decide who this person is and where he/she is located. Everything else is done is flashback/memory mode, using a split stage format. The person telling the story is on one side of the stage; all scenes that come from his/her memory are on the other side. This area, which I'll call the neutral zone, can become whatever you need it to be.

The group, other than the person narrating, plays multiple characters, i.e., the narrator's boss, spouse, lawyer, friend, teacher, etc. You should have at least three or four critical episodes in the person's life, ranging from early life to later life, depending on the age of the narrator. The scene should switch back and forth between the narrator and the episodes. What works best is to have a variety of people, at different ages, involved in a variety of circumstances or situations. The starting point for the scene is the emotional and physical space of the person telling the story. This scene should be appropriately scripted and practiced.

20. The Story of a Person's Life, Same Character

This one is essentially a monologue told by three people who are playing the same character, at different times in that person's life. It should not be performed as separate monologues, however. The story (monologues) must be communicated in fragments, and the dialogue is often overlapping. Three students create a single character and convey her life during critical stages. Keep in mind that a person's attitude or perspective changes throughout her lifetime.

The stage needs to be divided into three separate areas, one for each person. It's important to "dress" each area to reflect the given age of the character. The creative—and also challenging part of the scene—is "how" you communicate the story. The scene (script) needs to be written in a pattern, such as the following:

1. The scene begins with an old person reflecting on her past, speaking a couple of sentences.
2. At one point (I call this a "transitional" line) the old person and the child on stage speak at the same time, most likely the same words but, of course, with different meaning.
3. Now the child speaks a sentence or two.
4. The scene shifts back to the old person.
5. Transition line in which the old person and the middle age person speak the same words, in their different perspectives.
6. Now the middle age person speaks.
7. Transition line in which all three characters speak the same words.
8. The scene shifts back to the old person.
9. Transition line in which the middle age person and child speak the same words.
10. Now, once again, they all speak at the same time.
11. The scene shifts back to the old person.
12. Transition line in which the old person and child speak the same words.
13. Now the child speaks.

14. Transition line in which the child and middle age person speak the same words.
15. Now the middle age person speaks.
16. Now, once again, they all speak at the same time.
17. The scene shifts back to the old person.

The above pattern is only an example. Dozens, if not hundreds, of patterns exist, as you can imagine. This assignment requires an excellent script and precise timing and execution in the delivery of the scene. It's imperative to create a character with a compelling life story. Aim for irony or contrast between what one expected (perhaps at an early age) and what one received. Include surprises along the way. No person should have a predictable life from childhood to old age. When your character is not speaking, you should be frozen in a position that is revealing. In addition, when you do speak you need to bring your story "out" to the audience.

21. Three People, Same Story, Different Locations

For this scene, the stage is divided into three areas. Each character occupies his own space, which is a location/environment. Each of the characters stays in a freeze until he speaks. It is important to create variety in character, setting, story, tone, mood and emotion from person to person. Here's an example of a possible story: A husband, wife and detective are on stage, in different spaces. The husband is in his office, at work. The detective is standing in the rain, holding an umbrella. The wife is sitting in a café, sipping coffee, waiting for someone.

A pattern similar to the one used in "The Story of a Person's Life" must be used. In other words, the stories must intersect one another. Blending of voices must be used frequently. Sometimes the characters might say the same line at the same time or speak their own lines at the same time. Use an unpredictable pattern.

The characters do not have to be limited to their spaces all the time. They may enter each other's spaces during the dialogue. For instance, at one point, the detective may enter the husband's area and have a brief dialogue, and then go back to his area, standing in the rain. Anything is possible, as long as you avoid monologues. Limit each person's speaking parts to lines and words before switching to a new person. While I gave an example of a pattern in the previous assignment, it's impossible to place this one into a formula. None exist.

Of course, the scene can't be merely technique. You must have a compelling story, with intriguing characters. Certain types of genres work well for this assignment. Some of the best scenes I've seen have fallen into the category of mystery, suspense or horror.

22. Scene in Reverse

This scene is an experiment in narrative structure, less so in dialogue (as the previous two scenes). In traditional scenes, we see a beginning, middle and end (in that sequence). For this scene, you should begin with the end and finish with the beginning. The overall scene should be divided into three parts:

- The end (90 seconds)
- The middle (90 seconds)
- The beginning (90 seconds)

Your ending scene should be compelling enough to make us want to know what preceded it (what led up to this dramatic climax). In other words, what were the causes behind the actions and motives in the final scene. What works best for this one is using irony. In other words, given what happens in the beginning, we're surprised by the ending. Often times, events and actions are not what we expected. Avoid the usual response.

As is always the case, having a good story is paramount to making the scene effective. Once you have the story, you must place a "reverse spin" on it. Do not confuse reverse with rewind. The dialogue in each moment should be sequential.

This scene usually works best with three people. Each person doesn't necessarily have to be in each of the three moments, but the relationships between the three people and the motives behind their actions must be clear, whatever phase of the story.

AFTERWORD

What I offer in this book is the summation of my 23 years as a drama teacher. These pages contain the depth and breath—and fulfillment—of my experiences with students in my classroom. For me, these exercises, dialogues, improvisations and assignments have been effective tools not only as daily lessons, but, more importantly, as communicators to help me discover the hearts, minds and souls of my students. Therefore, I am excited to share my experiences and ideas with you. Drama, in all fairness, needs to be seen and heard, not described in words.

However, since this medium is available and convenient both to you and me, I gladly communicate what I've learned and what I know, from trial and error and constant experimentation. I hope that you, the reader/teacher, are able to decipher and extract what is most useful to you. If you're a teacher, at any level of experience, you know the importance of reading, researching and borrowing from as many sources as you can. Borrow freely as you continue to develop and grow in your love for teaching, and in your motivation to enrich your students' lives.

ABOUT THE AUTHOR

Thomas Crockett taught drama at El Camino High School in South San Francisco for 23 years, having directed 46 plays and musicals during his tenure there. While he plans to continue his passion for teaching acting and improvisation and directing plays, he desires, as well, to pursue related interests, such as writing plays and fiction. He has written a collection of short stories, *Hope Beyond All Hope*; a novel, *The Right Bus to Heaven,* and two full-length plays, *The Burrow People* and *A Tyrant For All Seasons*. Born and bred in New York, Mr. Crockett has lived in California for 30 years.

Made in the USA
Middletown, DE
07 August 2024